THE QUEST FOR EXCELLENCE

The Neo-Conservative Critique of Educational Mediocrity

NORMAN R.

(Photograph by Joe Pounder)

NORMAN R. PHILLIPS

Dr. Phillips is associate professor in the department of social sciences at Truman College of the City Colleges of Chicago. He has written extensively on the philosophy of conservatism and related subjects for such magazines and journals as the *Journal of Politics*, the *Mankind Quarterly*, *Modern Age*, the *National Review*, the *South Atlantic Quarterly*, and the *Western Political Quarterly*. His research findings have been widely utilized by other scholars.

During an extensive educational career, Dr. Phillips has taught on every level from kindergarten to graduate school.

He has been elected to membership in numerous professional associations including most recently the Philadelphia Society, a more conservative counterpart of the famous Ripon Society, and Phi Delta Kappa, professional educational fraternity.

Dr. Phillips studied at Roosevelt University, Northwestern University, Loyola University, and the University of Chicago.

THE QUEST FOR EXCELLENCE
THE NEO-CONSERVATIVE CRITIQUE
OF EDUCATIONAL MEDIOCRITY

by

Norman R. Phillips, Ph.D.
Associate Professor, Truman College
City Colleges of Chicago

Philosophical Library
New York

The author dedicates this book
to the memory of his mother

TABLE OF CONTENTS

Acknowledgments

In a book of the scope of the present work, it would be impossible to specify all the influences which have served to enlarge the viewpoint of the author.

The writer, however, wishes to express his gratitude to those scholars who have read the manuscript and given him the benefit of their reactions: Professors Gerald L. Gutek, Walter P. Krolikowski, and Rosemary V. Donatelli of Loyola University (Chicago) and Professor Edmund Dehnert of Truman College of the City Colleges of Chicago. The writer has also derived benefit from conversations with Professors Eliseo Vivas of Northwestern University (Evanston) and Thomas Wren of Loyola University.

Finally, a word of appreciation to the administrative and editorial staff of Philosophical Library for seeing this work through to completion.

Gateway Editions Limited has taken over publication rights to all books written by Dr. Russell Kirk which were originally published by the Henry Regnery Company. They have given me permission to make the extensive quotations from Professor Kirk's works appearing in this book.

Harcourt Brace Jovanovich Inc. has given me permission to quote extensively from *Christianity and Culture* by T. S. Eliot. All such quotations are cited and credited in the text.

It seems almost unnecessary to add that the author accepts full responsibility for the findings made and the conclusions reached in this study.

N. R. P.

THE QUEST FOR EXCELLENCE

CHAPTER I

THE MEANING AND SIGNIFICANCE OF NEO-CONSERVATISM

There is a widespread impression today among educated Americans that the American experiment in mass education has proven to be a failure. It is a well known fact that average ACT scores of college entrants have been declining over at least the past decade while there has, over the same period of time, been an overall rise in grade point averages of American high school and college students. In addition, American educational strivings have not resulted in the degree of cultural appreciation and, in non-technological areas, in the kind of intellectual and cultural productivity that was once so fondly expected. To cite two indicators of these facts, in contrast to the situations in nations like Great Britain, Germany, and Japan, bookstores are still relatively uncommon in the United States in spite of the greater amount of formal education available to the inhabitants of this country. In addition, to cite one area of intellectual achievement, philosophy, the United States evidently reached the peak of its recognized achievements at the turn of the century and in spite of the greater prevalence of mass education since that time has been on the decline ever since.

At that time, such influential philosophers as Dewey, James, Peirce, Royce, and Santayana were alive and flourishing on the American scene. Regardless of whether they deserved this fate or not, American philosophers since that time have not exerted the same degree of influence upon their compeers. A similar deliquescence with perhaps somewhat different dating can be observed in historical and fictional writing as well as in social and political theory.

Admittedly, there are other contributory causes for at least some of these trends. Yet, it is becoming strikingly evident that American education has been unable to counteract these tendencies. It is therefore high time to question and test the fundamental ideological assumptions upon which American educational practice has generally been based. American education is today governed ideologically by the actions of and the interactions between the proponents of a pragmatic utilitarianism, usually educational administrators, and advocates of various varieties of educational progressivism, usually faculty members. In spite of their internal differences, American educators have, on the whole, publicly favored the ideal of greater relative equality and have been somewhat suspicious of learning that is abstract, complex, and not attuned to the alleged needs of the masses. Many of them have also espoused the need for greater permissiveness in classroom practices and in the awarding of grades. As a viewpoint in diametrical opposition to all of these varied tendencies, educational conservatism is today very much on the defensive—even in quarters where it is properly understood. Yet, by calling the basic assumptions of American education into question, the educational conservatives merit our close attention; for by analyzing their thought, we should be able to clarify the fundamental and often subconsciously accepted philosophical underpinnings of American education and, thus, to grasp what needs to be changed. In addition, as we shall see more clearly later, the neo-conservative program for restoring belief in absolute standards of value should be of concern to anyone alarmed over the contemporary spiritual condition of humanity.

The Task

Specifically, this study seeks to ascertain the implications of neo-conservatism, the dominant contemporary form of conservative thought, pertaining to educational values and instructional means of imparting these values. For the purpose of this study, values will be construed to refer to general goods which can act as the guides and goals of human behavior. We will be especially concerned with intellectual and with moral values as well as with the standards of valuation which conservatives use to evaluate and judge educational outcomes. We will also give consideration to those neo-conservative recommendations which are designed to bring educational procedures into closer conformity with these standards.

Essentially, this study examines the writings of representative neo-conservative writers in historical perspective. As such, it is intended to be a work of intellectual history.[1] By analyzing the thoughts of prominent exponents of neo-conservatism, the conclusions we will reach will be based on more solid evidence than mere conjectures. By relating our conclusions to current historical trends, we can make important inferences on the causes and significance of the neo-conservative movement.

It is because conservatism has powerfully influenced the destiny of man and of nations that it is entitled to be of major concern to the historian. As the dominant philosophy of many of the elites of the past, it is an essential in the understanding of many of the most important events of the past as well as of contemporary dilemmas. In addition, a philosophy which has commanded the allegiance of many of the most influential intellectuals of history from Pythagoras and Plato to contemporary figures like T. S. Eliot and Oswald Spengler cannot easily be ignored by anyone who wishes to understand intellectual history.[2]

No attempt will be made to analyze the popular usage of "conservatism" which has been confused and inconsistent in nature. The term has been used in such varied ways that it is difficult to discern a common trend; having been applied on various occasions to everything from Southern populists to aristocratic authoritarians. It is hoped that this book will contribute to a more precise formulation of the concept of conservatism.

This study will consider the educational implications of neo-conservative thought by surveying those conservative writers who have done a substantial analysis of educational issues to enable us to form a conception of their general educational viewpoint. In addition, only those writers will be discussed whose writings are on a level above that of invective, vituperation, and mere polemics. The following conservative writers will be emphasized in this study: Irving Babbitt, G. H. Bantock, Bernard Iddings Bell, T. S. Eliot, and Russell Kirk. Three of these writers, Babbitt, Eliot, and Kirk, have probably had a greater influence on neo-conservatism than any other neo-conservative writers.

Since an essentially historical approach will be utilized, the ideas to be analyzed will be viewed in relationship to the particular problems of the age in which they were expounded—both in respect to the causes which led to the advocacy of these ideas and the significance thereof. To demonstrate the boundaries of this inquiry, it is essential to define conservatism and to show how neo-conservatism differs from other kinds of conservatism.

4

To define a concept adequately, a writer should first give some indication of his method for arriving at a definition. We could take common usage as the basis for a definition but this immediately leads to difficulties. As we have seen, there has been very little consistency in the way the term "conservative" has been employed in common usage. Alternative definitions may be derived from the usage of persons trained in fields where conceptual discrimination is important, but, as will be evident shortly, such definitions have generally been inadequate. A more promising technique is to examine the contextual usage of "conservative" and of cognate terms by scholars to discover the logic behind their usage. Historical evidence will be cited but since the meanings of general concepts tends to vary with the *Zeitgeist*, this evidence will not be overly stressed.

The most common definition of conservatism used by scholars is the disposition to preserve whatever has been established. This common definition lacks discriminative value because if it is applied consistently, then the Marxist in Russia, the Fascist in Spain, and the liberal in the United States would all have to be labelled "conservative." Such imprecise usage tends to make conservatism synonomous with either conformity or opportunism. This is so contrary to the way political and social theorists generally use the conservative appellation that it scarcely merits serious consideration. In fact, contemporary conservatives in the United States are generally very dissatisfied with the general liberal character of American society. The ounce of truth in this definition relates to the conservative advocacy of tradition, but, as we shall see later, this traditionalism pertains only to those elements of the cultural heritage which have survived for many centuries and only when these elements harmonize with other aspects of conservatism.

5

Another definition which has gained wide currency was originally offered by Russell Kirk. Unfortunately, Professor Kirk did not give us an analytical definition but rather a list of symptoms of conservatism. By analyzing this definition, we should however be able to arrive at a more precise conception of the essence of conservatism; especially if we consider how widely his definition has been accepted by intellectuals. Kirk's definition consists of six planks which we will give in order and then analyze.

"(1) A belief in an order that is more than human which has implanted in man a character of mingled good and evil, susceptible of improvement only by an inner working, not by mundane schemes for perfectability. This conviction lies at the heart of American respect for the past, as the record of Providential purpose. The conservative mind is suffused with veneration. Men and nations, the conservative believes, are governed by moral laws, and political problems, at bottom, are moral and religious problems. An eternal chain of duties links the generations that are dead, and the generation that is living now, and the generations yet to be born. We have no right, in this brief existence of ours, to alter irrevocably the shape of things, in contempt of our ancestors and of the rights of posterity. Politics is the art of apprehending and applying the justice which stands above statutory law.

"(2) An affection for variety and complexity and individuality, even for singularity, which has exerted a powerful check upon the political tendency toward what Tocqueville calls 'democratic despotism.' Variety and complexity, in the opinion of conservatives, are the high gifts of truly civilized society. The uniformity and standardization of liberal and radical planners would be the death of vitality and freedom, a life-in-death, every man precisely like his neighbor—and, like the damned of the *inferno*, forever deprived of hope.

"(3) A conviction that justice properly defined, means 'to each the things that go with his own nature,' not a levelling equality; and joined with this is a correspondent respect for private property of every sort. Civilized society requires distinctions of order, wealth, and responsibility; it cannot exist without true leadership. A free society will endeavor, indeed, to afford to men of natural abilities every opportunity to rise by their own efforts, but it will resist strenuously the radical delusion that exact equality of station and wealth can benefit everyone. Society longs for just leadership, and if people destroy natural distinctions among men, presently some Bonaparte will fill the vacuum—or worse than Bonaparte.

"(4) A suspicion of concentrated power, and a consequent attachment to our federal principle and to division and balancing of authority at every level of government.

"(5) A reliance upon private endeavor and sagacity in nearly every walk of life, together with a contempt for the abstract designs of the collectivistic reformer. But to this self-reliance in the mind of the American conservative, is joined the conviction that in matters beyond the scope of material endeavor and the present moment, the individual tends to be foolish, but the species is wise; therefore, we rely in great matters upon the wisdom of our ancestors. History is an immense storehouse of knowledge. We pay a decent respect to the moral traditions and immemorial customs of mankind; for men who ignore the past are condemned to repeat it. The conservative distrusts the radical visionary and the planner who would chop society into pieces and mold it nearer to his heart's desire. The conservative appeals beyond the fickle opinion of the hour to what Chesterton called 'the democracy of the dead'—that is, the considered judgment of the wise men who died before our time. To presume that men can plan rationally the whole of existence is to expose mankind to a terrible danger from the

7

collapse of existing institutions; for, conservatives know that most men are governed, on many occasions, more by emotion than by pure reason.

"(6) A prejudice against organic change, a feeling that it is unwise to break radically with political prescription, an inclination to tolerate what abuses may exist in present institutions out of a practical acquaintanceship with the violent and unpredictable nature of doctrinaire reform."[3]

Although Kirk's definition contains much impassioned rhetoric and imprecision, it nevertheless reveals fundamental conservative attitudes. These attitudes become more evident when his six points are rearranged into two broad general categories: the first of which pertains to man's weakness and irrational nature and his consequent need for traditional authority; the second, to the desirability of an aristocratic, elitist social order. Points two and three relate to the second category, the other four points of Kirk's definition to the first category.

Concerning the first category, Kirk began his definition of conservatism with an expression of skepticism concerning schemes for the perfection of humanity. He felt that men could not plan rationally for the future of other men because of their own irrationality which he blamed on their alleged emotionalism. Because of this doubt, Kirk preferred to rely on private endeavor with respect to matters of limited scope, and on traditional wisdom, with regard to matters of greater scope. Evidently, because of this same basic distrust of human nature, he advocated the division and balancing of political powers.

With regard to the second category, Kirk advocated the encouragement of variety because of his evident fear of a dead-level equalitarianism and advocated proportionate rather than equalitarian justice because of the need for true leadership. He felt that men must have leaders, and, if these

8

are not selected consciously, leaders would arise anyway but of a rather undesirable type.

It seems evident from the preceding analysis that the essential features of Kirk's conservatism were the advocacy of an aristocratic elitism and of traditional authority. In these respects, Kirk was typical of conservative thinkers as a group. Ultimately, the aristocratic side of conservatism was based upon a conception of the universe as rationally ordered in a hierarchical pattern of superordination and subordination. This conception was in fundamental accord with the British Tories' insistence that each individual should find the place in the social hierarchy most suitable to him and should be content with it. Traditional conservatism was based partially on an acute consciousness of the moral and intellectual limitations of the individual and partially upon a belief in the superiority of tradition as a standard of judgment based upon the collective experience of generations of human beings. These points will be discussed in greater detail in the second chapter where the conservative viewpoint will be analyzed and its implications developed.

Conservatism therefore should be considered to be that social philosophy whose advocates espouse an aristocratic elitism and also stress the value of traditional authority. The adjective, aristocratic, refers in this instance both to a hierarchical conception of values and to a hierarchical conception of humanity. Because of this viewpoint, conservatism is elitist in the sense that conservatives traditionally have advocated rule by a select group and have stressed the importance of the careful selection and training of elite groups in all the major realms of human endeavor. Conservative traditionalism in turn has been based upon an acute consciousness of the limitations of the individual together with a belief in the value of the collective experience of peoples and nations. Ultimately, the most essential ingredient in the conservative constellation of beliefs is the hierarchical conception of reality. Not only is the aristocratic aspect of conservatism based upon hierarchy but also, in part, the traditional aspect as well. Has not the conservative's consciousness of human limitations been based to some extent on his conception of the place of humans in the hierarchy of the universe? Also, as we shall see later, traditional authority was considered to be a means whereby the fruits of excellence could be protected against the menace of revolution. More than any other word, "order" is symbolic of the essence of conservatism. Order stands for the Hierarchical arrangement of the universe and for the importance of authority in human affairs.

It is important to distinguish conservatism from classical liberalism with which it is often confused. Indeed, classical liberalism is in many respects opposed to conservatism. It has become customary to confuse classical liberalism with conservatism—especially in the United States but also to a lesser degree in other countries. Such confusion can easily lead to a neglect of the peculiar excellences of each of these viewpoints. To the classical liberal, the primary objective of government is the protection and enhancement of the liberties of the people. In contrast, although the conservative recognizes the value of freedom, he deems it to be secondary to the attainment and preservation of order in both senses of the term—both respect for authority and encouragement of a hierarchical ordering of society. In addition, the classical liberal is committed to the advocacy of a free market economy while the conservative, in spite of a few distinguished exceptions like Edmund Burke, generally is agreeable to a moderate amount of government control. Perhaps the most salient contrast between classical liberals and conservatives pertains to their attitudes toward tradition and the aristocratic viewpoint. While conservatives champion traditional authority, classical liberals are more likely to advocate the removal of traditional barriers to free competition. Furthermore, classical liberals tend to be democratic rather than aristocratic in their social philosophy. Even when they evince elitist tendencies, as in the case of the social Darwinians, they tend to have faith in the processes of natural selection in the recruitment of elites, while conservatives are much more likely to favor formal means of selection. Finally, conservatives generally favor the encouragement of organized religion while classical liberals either oppose such encouragement or seek to keep their religious and political viewpoints separate from one another.

To a considerable extent, the differences between classical liberals and conservatives relate to their differing views of human nature. Traditionally, the leading expositors of classical liberalism have tended to view man as essentially selfish but rational. Because of their selfishness, men could be depended upon to strive for their own self-interest. Because of their alleged rationality, they would be considered to be consistent in striving for this goal. Thus, if they were to be left alone to strive for their own selfish goods, the good of society as a whole would be advanced. On the other hand, because of human selfishness, governments must be limited in their powers for governments are made up of human beings, all of whom possess this type of character. In contrast, while the conservatives would agree that human beings are selfish, they would also maintain that most people, at least, are irrational. Hence, they would evince less faith in the automatic workings of a free society.

If classical liberals like Herbert Hoover and Barry Goldwater are today often confused with conservatives, this confusion is probably due to the fact that both groups have tended to unite on certain issues in common opposition to the doctrines espoused by adherents of doctrines of both the extreme and moderate Left. This unity is based upon

11

the common opposition of both groups to schemes of collectivistic social reform. Classical liberals oppose these plans
because they consider them to be menaces to freedom;
conservatives, because they consider them to be equalitarian in tendency.

Historically, conservatives and classical liberals were on
opposing sides until well into the twentieth century. In fact,
the term "conservative" acquired its present meaning in the
early nineteenth century when it was used to designate
those individuals and groups which opposed the principles
associated with the French Revolution. These conservatives
were aristocratic, traditionalist, and generally favorable to
the mercantilist economic principles that were still dominant in much of Europe. Their chief opponents were the
liberals who at that time championed progressivism and
laissez-faire. These liberals would now be regarded as adherents of classical liberalism in contradistinction to the adherents of the social democratic liberalism of today, who are
prepared to accept a considerable amount of government
control in the pursuit of their objectives. Conservatism is, of
course, much older than the French Revolution for essentially the same principles were expounded by Pythagoras.[4]
It is of considerable significance that modern conservatism
was originally directed primarily in opposition to classical
liberalism, a philosophy with which conservatism has recently been frequently confused.

It is symptomatic of the confusion of terms that is so
prevalent today that Michael Oakeshott has been frequently labeled a conservative. Yet, if we examine his interpretation of conservatism carefully, we cannot fail to notice how
divergent it is from the views of the major expositors of
conservatism and how similar it is to the views of classical
liberal writers in general. As far as Oakeshott was concerned, conservatism was purely a political doctrine without any
entailments pertaining to the nature of man. This in itself

12

would have astonished such distinguished conservatives as Edmund Burke, Prince Metternich, and Samuel Taylor Coleridge. Oakeshott placed the essence of conservatism in the belief that government should confine itself to keeping the peace and regulating the currency. It was not to indulge itself in social reform. As far as he was concerned, happiness could only come through the voluntary and free choices of the individual. On the basis of this position, Oakeshott should be classified as a classical liberal rather than a conservative. His paramount political value was obviously freedom rather than order. He should therefore be placed in the same ideological camp with Adam Smith and Friedrich Hayek rather than in the camp of Edmund Burke and Benjamin Disraeli.[5]

To establish the precise parameters of this study, it is important to consider briefly other viewpoints which have sometimes been confused with conservatism. They include the views of Admiral Hyman Rickover whose educational elitism would link him to the conservative position but whose main concern has been to recruit academic talent suited to grapple with contemporary problems rather than to reassert the values of the past. In American educational history, there has also been a considerable number of influential thinkers who have espoused the values of a traditional liberal arts education and, at the same time, have rejected the aristocratic viewpoint which has traditionally been associated with this kind of education. They include the perennialists, Robert W. Hutchins and Mortimer J. Adler. Hutchins, in particular, has publicly taken an anti-Burkean position and has attacked T. S. Eliot because of the aristocratic proclivities of the latter.[6] Russell Kirk was undoubtedly at least partially correct in viewing Hutchins as a democratic rationalist; for Hutchins has tended to emphasize critical independent thought combined with a strong faith in democratic values, both in politics and in

13

education.[7] Mortimer Adler has evinced a similar reliance upon democratic values in education in contradistinction to the aristocratic values espoused by conservatives, even to the extent of advocating mass college education.[8] Neither individual has been commonly regarded by conservative intellectuals as representative of their viewpoint; for, like the classical liberals, the perennialists resemble the conservatives in some respects but differ greatly from them in other equally important ways. These two schools appear to be allied only when contrasted to those schools which are characterized by a more relativistic and less academic approach than either. In much the same manner, the similarities between conservatives and classical liberals become vividly apparent when contrasted with the socialists and other variants of the political Center and Left. But we must not let the similarities blind us to the differences lest we overlook the peculiar values of each viewpoint.

In addition to Hutchins and Adler, there have been many other writers on education who have eagerly espoused the benefits of an academic liberal arts education and, at the same time, have shied away from the aristocratic ethos with which such an education has been traditionally associated. This has been especially true of American writers. Such primary figures as William Chandler Bagley and Arthur Bestor, Jr. have established this combination of attitudes and, unlike Hutchins and Adler, they have also opposed traditionalism—preferring to justify their educational programs on utilitarian grounds.[9] In this respect, Bestor has not exhibited the same faith in the educability of the masses as has Bagley but his antipathy to traditionalistic concepts of education has been no less unequivocal. In general, the American cultural atmosphere has not been very conducive to the emergence of an aristocratic traditionalism; for a landed aristocracy that might have served as a model and support for this viewpoint has never become

14

firmly established on American soil. In addition, in so new a nation sufficient time has not elapsed for the development of a strong and efficacious traditionalism. Seen in such a light, the neo-conservative movement is a radical departure from the established American way of life.

There has been at least as much confusion over the question of how neo-conservatism differs from conservatism proper as there has been over the meaning of conservatism itself. Some writers deny any difference; they look upon neo-conservatism as simply a revival of traditional conservatism.[10] Others, including a number of writers on education have contrasted the humanism of Irving Babbitt and his associates with the allegedly "new conservatism" of the Council for Basic Education which in turn has been linked to the old theory of formal discipline.[11] The humanists were allegedly exponents of the inculcation of certain ethical and aesthetic ideals while the neo-conservatives were more interested in educational methods—especially in methods of training mental faculties. Actually, the facts do not support this distinction. As we shall see later, humanist ideals are as important to the neo-conservatives of today as to Irving Babbitt and his supporters. Furthermore, instead of separating Babbitt's humanism from contemporary conservatism, it would be more correct to view both as part of one movement in response to the same basic pressures, the gap being bridged by the existence of two short-lived but influential magazines; *The American Review* (1933-1937) and *Measure* (1949-1950). Furthermore, the Council on Basic Education has hardly been confined to conservatives but has also included people representing a wide range of educational opinion such as the disciples of William Bagley and of Admiral Hyman Rickover.

In actuality, the distinctiveness of the new conservatism does not lie in any originality but rather in a difference of emphasis as compared with traditional conservatism. Modern conservatism first arose as a response to the excesses of the French Revolution. As the first influential spokesman of modern conservatism, Edmund Burke defended the status quo against a primarily political menace. Twentieth century conservatives can no longer defend the status quo for their principles no longer dominate any important Western society. Instead, they advocate reform—but reform in a vastly different direction from what either the liberals or radicals recommend. Furthermore, the neo-conservatives are today primarily concerned with educational and intellectual rather than political matters. They are therefore primarily cultural critics of the age. Two trends have particularly aroused their fears. One of these has been the gradual erosion of religious and moral beliefs which, at least in part, was undoubtedly the outcome of attacks on specific religious dogmas by such figures as Copernicus and Darwin. The second tendency has been the gradual replacement of academic values and standards of selective education by an increasing stress upon mass culture which was apparently itself a by-product of both the decline of tradition and the spread of democratic as against aristocratic values. This second tendency has been most pronounced in the United States which might explain the high proportion of Americans among neo-conservative writers. The high percentage of academics and intellectuals found within this group might be an indication of a fear of trends which would undermine the status of intellectuals and of their values; for the disinterested pursuit of intellectual excellence is sometimes difficult to maintain in a milieu in which mass appeal is the touchstone.

Among contemporary conservative thinkers, the views of two writers on the causes of the perlexities of the contemporary age have been especially influential.[12] One of these was the late Richard Weaver, a professor of English at the University of Chicago. He traced the present decline in

16

moral and intellectual standards back to William of Ockham's denial of the reality of the Platonic universals back in the fourteenth century. This rejection led ultimately to the denial of the existence of a source of truth higher than man. The consequences included the spread of ethical relativism, metaphysical skepticism, and the concomitant repudiation of cultural standards. For Weaver, the problem of the contemporary age was of how to enable humans to again perceive an ordered hierarchy of values.[13]

An especially outspoken critic of contemporary thought was Eric Voegelin, who has been Director of the Institute for Political Science at the University of Munich. Central to Voegelin's approach to contemporary problems was the contrast he made between the political "science" which according to Voegelin typified both Plato and Aristotle and the so-called gnostic approach of recent writers. Voegelin characterized Plato and Aristotle as engaged in the search for the order of being, which order dissatisfied the "gnostics." The latter wanted to replace this order with a man-centered one, thereby denying the existence of a transcendent source of being and order. Among the movements which Voegelin characterized as being gnostic were national socialism, fascism, Marxism, Freudianism, progressivism, and positivism. The adherents of all of these movements had in effect denied the validity of faith, preferring to rely on their own special brands of "knowledge" and on earthly forms of salvation. The remedy that he recommended was to somehow restore faith in a transcendent order of being.[14]

In spite of their obvious differences in approach, both Weaver and Voegelin saw the ills of the modern world as due fundamentally to the repudiation of the existence of a hierarchical order of goods and the remedy thereof in the revival of belief in such an order, although neither writer was very explicit on how this was to be attained. The writings of both of these men provides an insight into the neo-conservative approach to contemporary problems. In their hopes and fears, Weaver and Voegelin were typical of many neo-conservative writers.

In brief, our task will be to analyze the writings of those neo-conservatives who have written extensive and serious expositions of their educational views and who had some influence on other conservatives and on educators in general. The purpose will be to uncover the educational aims and methods implicit in the neo-conservative ideology. By treating this matter historically, on the basis of past writings in relationship to the *Zeitgeist*, it is hoped that a better understanding will be obtained of the ultimate significance of conservative educational thought in relationship to the various forms of educational liberalism and progressivism. Before we can deal directly with this subject, it is important that we analyze the fundamental assumptions and presuppositions of neo-conservative writers pertaining to the nature of the universe and of man's place therein.

NOTES

[1] For a discussion of the meanings of intellectual history see H. Stuart Hughes, *Consciousness and Society* (New York: Alfred A. Knopf, 1958), pp. 9-10.

[2] On the role of Plato, see Norman R. Phillips, "An Historical Understanding of Conservatism," *The National Review* 21 (March 25, 1969), pp. 279-281, 297.

[3] Quoted from Russell Kirk, *A Program for Conservatives* (Chicago: Henry Regnery Company, 1954), pp. 41-43.

[4] For a discussion of the place of Pythagoras in the history of conservative thought see Carroll Quigley, *The Evolution of Civilizations* (New York: MacMillan, 1961), pp. 186-188, 196-197.

[5]For evidences of Michael Oakeshott's views on conservatism see his *Rationalism In Politics and Other Essays* (London: Metheun, 1962), especially pages 183, 189, 191. Incidentally, in spite of his denial, his political views most certainly entail certain definite views pertaining to both human nature and the nature of the universe.

[6]Russell Kirk has listed the writings by Hutchins in which these views were expressed in Kirk's *Eliot and His Age* (New York: Random House, 1971), pp. 357-358.

[7]Kirk's characterization of Hutchins can be found in Kirk's *Academic Freedom* (Chicago: Henry Regnery Company, 1955), p. 74.

[8]See Adler's essay in Robert Hemenway, ed., *A Great Books Primer* (Chicago: Great Books Foundation, 1955), pp. 25-27.

[9]Bagley's general position is generally familiar to students of his philosophy. For examples of Bestor's viewpoint see his *The Restoration of Learning* (New York: Alfred A. Knopf, 1955), pp. 48, 87, 94.

[10]See for example Edward N. Burns and Philip L. Ralph, *World Civilizations* (New York: W. W. Norton Company, 1968), Vol. 2, p. 699. In this generally accurate text, the authors have also erroneously classified the classical liberal economist, Friedrich Hayek, as a conservative.

[11]See for example, John P. Wynne, *Theories of Education* (New York: Harper and Row, 1963), pp. 401, 492, 498-499.

[12]As evidenced by the spate of articles on both of these writers which have appeared in such conservative journals as *Modern Age* and *The Intercollegiate Review*. A Richard M. Weaver Fellowship Awards Program has been established by the right-wing Intercollegiate Studies Institute.

[13]Richard Weaver, *Ideas have Conseqeunces* (Chicago: University of Chicago Press, 1948), pp. 2-3, 19-20.

[14]See especially Eric Voegelin, *Science, Politics, and Gnosticism* (Chicago: Henry Regnery Company, 1968), pp. 15-18, 86-88.

CHAPTER II

PHILOSOPHICAL FOUNDATIONS OF NEO-CONSERVATISM

In substance, neo-conservatism constitutes a social philosophy in the broadest sense of the term. It is a philosophy which describes the nature of society including man's place therein and also prescribes definite policies both for the good of the individual and of society as a whole. It also implies a characteristic viewpoint pertaining to the nature of being and of the universe. This chapter will explore the fundamental neo-conservative concepts pertaining to the nature of the universe, man, and society as a means of preparing a foundation for the explication of the neo-conservative educational viewpoint to follow. Since, as was pointed out in the first chapter, neo-conservatism differs from traditional conservatism only in emphasis, the basic doctrinal assumptions of both are identical. Therefore, the terms "conservatism" and "neo-conservatism" will be used interchangeably.

The Concept of Hierarchy

Perhaps the most fundamental concept underlying the conservative philosophy is hierarchy; for the conservative tends to conceive of the universe in terms of a gradual unilinear gradation in contrast to both the single-level equalitarianism of the radicals and the two-layer elite-mass dichotomy stressed by the fascists. Historically, the conservative concept of hierarchy, at least as employed by writers belonging to Occidental cultures, was largely derived from and stated in the terminology of Aristotle. Through two influential British Aristotelians, Richard Hooker and Edmund Burke, this concept became fundamental to the conservatism of the English-speaking countries. It is therefore important to discuss Aristotle's views on hierarchy.

Although Aristotle has given us several systems of gradation, the one which most fundamentally influenced Western metaphysics pertained to the powers of the soul. To Aristotle, the soul was a property of living organisms which enable them to function as well as the functioning thereof. Thus, all living things were characterized as having nutritive powers. In addition to these powers, animals possessed the powers of movement and of sensation. Such cognitive powers as imagination and memory were considered to be outgrowths of the sensitive soul. Finally, humans possessed, in addition to all the powers characteristics of plants and animals, the faculty of reason. All living things, with the exception of God, were deemed to be imperfect in the sense that none fully actualized all the potentialities of all living things. Aristotle felt that all living things belonged to a hierarchy in accordance with the degree to which they actualized the potentialities of living things as a whole. Finally, happiness for each living thing was believed to consist in performing well the characteristic function by which it was distinguished from other creatures in the scale of nature.[1]

At first glance, this hierarchy appears to apply largely to different genera and species of living things rather than to intraspecific differences such as those between humans but it is actually but a short step to transfer such a concept from interspecific to intraspecific differences. How this was done has been clearly exemplified in the writings of Sir Thomas Elyot, one of the early pioneers of conservative educational theory. Sir Thomas has pointed out that God has ordered all His creatures from the most inferior upwards; for everything is ordered since without order all would be chaos. What applies to the rest of creation must also apply to humanity; for God's providence applies to men as well as to the inferior creatures.[2] Thus, the same principle of order which was believed to characterize all creation was also applied to the differences between men.

This led to a conception of society as an ordered and interconnected whole bound together by a great all-embracing hierarchy in which the position of the individual was determined by the functions that he performed. Richard Hooker, who was one of the seminal thinkers of both British conservatism and of the Anglican Church, exemplified this attitude quite clearly in his writings. He believed that the whole world was compacted so that each thing performed only that work which was natural to it; for God set up a function for each creature. To forget one's function or to transgress it was deemed to be evil. Hooker even quoted Aristotle to the effect that there is a natural right of the noble and wise to govern those of servile disposition.[3] Thus, the characteristic outlook of many representatives of the British aristocracy that there is a place on the social hierarchy for each individual and that the common good is promoted when each individual knows his place in that society and performs his functions in society well. This structural-functional conception of society is diametrically opposed to the thorough individualism of the classical liberals who, in the United States, are often confused with conservatives.

At least as important as Aristotle's hierarchy of being was

his hierarchy of values; for Aristotle assumed that some values were intrinsically and objectively superior to others. Once such an assumption is granted, it is but a short step to the assumption that some men, as exemplars of these values, are superior to those who exemplify lesser values in their basic affinities and actions. By examining the standards employed by Aristotle and developed to a greater degree of explicitness by the man who was probably Aristotle's most influential disciple, St. Thomas Aquinas, we should be able to get a clear idea of the conservative criteria for the ranking of values. Such an examination is necessary because conservative writers on the whole have not been very explicit on this very important matter. Since Aristotle's metaphysics, as modified and interpreted by such medieval figures as St. Thomas, Hooker, and Elyot, have been dominant in conservative thought, it is likely that the Aristotelian-Thomistic axiology would provide us with a reasonably accurate guide to the fundamental value assumptions of conservatives. This procedure becomes especially cogent when we consider the prevalence of subjectivist conceptions of values among liberal and radical thinkers; for the Aristotelian-Thomistic axiology is not only objectivist in character but buttresses objectivist conceptions of value on cogent philosophical grounds.[4]

Instead of one all-embracing hierarchy, those who utilize the Aristotelian-Thomistic approach utilize several different hierarchies in accordance with the nature of the category to be considered. Thus, the value of justice would be tested by the equity and proportionateness of the acts or things being compared. Those which evidence the greatest proportionateness in relationship to one another would approach most closely to the ideal of pure justice.

A second class of virtues, distinct from justice, would consist of those moral traits, such as courage and temperance, which are characterized by self-discipline and self-

24

control. These virtues would be ranked both in terms of the degree of self-control needed and in terms of the ends for which self-control is exercised. Thus, St. Thomas rated courage as in general above temperance in the hierarchy of values since such an exercise of courage as the display of heroism in battle is much more demanding than, let us say, temperance in the consumption of alcoholic beverages. In general, these virtues are to be rated below justice and the intellectual virtues since these others should direct and control these particular moral virtues.

Of the intellectual virtues, which are those excellences pertaining to cognition, prudence would direct the moral virtues since it pertains to practical "wisdom" or the choice of means with respect to the ends perceived by the speculative intellect. Since the speculative intellect is concerned with the choice of ultimate ends, it should direct the exercise of prudence which in turn should regulate the moral virtues. Of the moral virtues, St. Thomas recognized justice as highest in rank since, to some extent, it should be regulative of the other moral virtues although presumably justice itself should be responsive to the exercise of the intellectual virtues.

As to which virtue ranks highest of all, the two virtues which have been most usually stressed by the ancient philosophers of both Hellas and the Far East have been wisdom and mystical or intuitive insight, although the two have often been subsumed under the same rubric since these both pertain to cognitive understanding and since intuition might simply be ratiocination which is so swift in its functioning as to seem immediate in character.

Aristotle ranked theoretical wisdom as the highest virtue while St. Thomas thought it to be the highest natural virtue.[5] Both men understood wisdom to embrace the understanding of first principles and what follows from first principles pertaining to the highest objects and the final

25

causes. The exercise of this virtue was thought to provide us with knowledge of the ends which should guide our conduct. In addition, Aristotle believed that theoretical wisdom provided the most lasting and intrinsically valuable satisfactions of which humans were capable. Among many others, Plato and Buddha also gave the highest rating to theoretical wisdom although they conceived of it in such a way as to merge the fruits of both mystical experience and theoretical reasoning, whereas this was not true of either Aristotle or St. Thomas, who viewed it more exclusively as the product of speculative reasoning.

St. Thomas, however, rated *caritas* as the highest of all virtues—natural or supernatural. Through *caritas*, man might hope, according to St. Thomas, to attain beatitude, the vision of God, which St. Thomas regarded as the final end and the most lasting satisfaction of man. Thus, through the motivating power of *caritas*, the most perfect power of human nature, the speculative intellect, is focused on the most perfect object to achieve the most perfect good. In this manner, St. Thomas has come very close indeed to the Eastern mystics whose highest good was the experiencing of the Godhead within the individual together with the contemplation and the understanding thereof.

One might ask why love was not included in the hierarchy of moral virtues. The answer lies in the nature of virtue. To both Aristotle and St. Thomas, virtue was the disposition toward the good; whereas love, as a passion, could be directed either toward the good or the evil depending on the object; for love is an emotional affinity and our evaluation of it must therefore vary with the worthiness of the objects of that affinity.

Our present concern with the hierarchy of values is, however, directed not so much to the nature of these values as to the methods used in ordering them. Our purpose is to show how, on conservative principles, we can erect a meaningful hierarchy of values which is dependent on something more objective and substantial than fickle human desires. In accordance with the general character of Aristotelian metaphysics, the hierarchy thus established is essentially a functional one which was based on a variety of standards but is dominated by a teleological ends-means network. Certain values were deemed to be means to other values until we reach those values considered to be intrinsically valuable in themselves. The determination of the ranking of these values was based on their functions, as ascertained by the essential natures of the values themselves, and as determined by their ultimate ends which were conceived of as wisdom by Aristotle and as a combination of wisdom (in the natural order) and of beatitude (in what transcends the natural order) by St. Thomas. In fact, there was a pronounced tendency on the parts of both these sages to rank ends in terms of their nearness to speculative wisdom on the assumption that wisdom is the supreme virtue of this temporal world which gives guidance to the exercise of the other values of the natural order. The general approach is symptomatic of the structural-functional viewpoint which has characterized conservative metaphysics although, as we shall see later, conservatives have as a group been unfortunately very vague concerning the nature and content of the value hierarchy which they espouse. They generally conceive of hierarchy in the same functional terms as did Aristotle, but they have not been very specific concerning its nature. Yet specificity is required if we are to solve the central problem of contemporary philosophy—how to provide an objective guide to the evaluation of human thoughts and actions. If they are to be consistent with their basic assumptions, the neo-conservatives need to espouse an axiology somewhat similar to what we have just outlined and discussed.

Among the many implications of the concept of hierarchy is the support which it gives to the existence of universal purpose and of a rational power who designed the universe to bring that purpose to fruition; for the affirmation of the existence of a hierarchical universe clearly implies belief in a rationally designed universe, ordered in terms of the superordination and subordination of its inhabitants and of the values they typify. Order implies rationality and rationality implies purpose. This viewpoint is congruent with the acceptance and espousal of religious beliefs and values. Therefore, while conservatives have undoubtedly evinced a tendency to be somewhat pessimistic concerning human nature, their essential metaphysical viewpoint implies a strong confidence in the meaningfulness and ultimate goodness of the cosmos.

In addition, since hierarchy implies diversity and since diversity is accepted as part of some great overall plan, then diversity itself must be good and every effort should be made to encourage it. Furthermore, since the universe contains beings at various stages of perfection, this implies that they are likewise at various stages of imperfection. Implicit in such a view is a theodicy; for evil as well as good are thus necessary to the fulfillment of the universal plan.

Metaphysical materialism is fundamentally antithetical to the hierarchical viewpoint, for the concept of a universe as consisting of matter in motion implies either a tychist or a mechanistic view of causation—both of which would exclude purpose as an integral feature of the cosmos. The inclusion of final causation as an ultimate explanation of universal phenomena clearly implies the existence of factors which transcend the blind operations of the physical universe. It is therefore scarcely surprising that conservative thinkers have generally been hostile to Marxianism and other forms of metaphysical Materialism. In this particular, their attitude has certainly been consistent with their basic metaphysical assumptions.

With regard to education, a quotation from the writings of Paul Elmer More, a literary critic and associate of Irving Babbitt, should give us a vivid comprehension of the viewpoint of the conservative intellectual.

"The scheme of the humanist might be described as the disciplining of the higher imagination to the end that the student may behold in one sublime vision, the whole scale of being in its range from the lowest to the highest under the divine decree of order and subordination, without losing sight of the immutable veracity at the heart of all development which is only the praise and surname of virtue."[6]

In more commonplace language, More was in effect advocating that the student learn to discriminate between the higher and the lower, the better and the worse, utilizing the universal hierarchy of being as the foundation of values. As to the "praise and surname of virtue," More explained this as being synonomous with the trait or quality of nobility.[7]

In more general terms, an emphasis upon hierarchy would obviously lead to a stress upon human differences, with the advocacy of different kinds of training in accordance with differences in the abilities and interests of the students involved. Furthermore, such an emphasis upon human variability would strengthen the position of those who believe that a considerable amount of formal education is not necessary to the fulfillment of all persons since human nature covers such a wide scope of aptitudes and interests that it would be difficult to find a single nostrum adequate for all.

Hierarchical views are conducive to aristocratic conceptions of education. Since all creatures are not equivalent in potentialities, there would presumably be a tendency to stress those with the greatest manifest potentiality on the ground that to do otherwise would result in the neglect of those most able to contribute to the progress of civilization. The emphasis upon unequal potentialities is crucial in this

29

respect; for one could acknowledge that men are not equal in actuality but still maintain that all or most men are equal in potentiality. A proponent of this view could then easily advocate mass education through the college level with attention focused on the development of students of only average manifest academic potentiality. Once one accepts the existence of important differences in potentialities between students, one is almost certain to accept the desirability of selective education with emphasis upon the training of the superior.

The religious implications of the concept of hierarchy should be encouraging to those concerned with religious and moral training in the schools. Also, the fact that conservatives tend to ground their values in an ordering of nature could conceivably lead to an educational sequence wherein the student would study the natural sciences first before he approaches religion and ethics. As has already been observed, an essential aim of education would be the development of the ability of the student to discriminate between the relative worth of the various constituent parts of the universe in terms of their position in the universal hierarchy. The acknowledgement of differences in intrinsic worth would obviously lead to a stress on philosophy, especially on those branches which pertain specifically to value—such as ethics and aesthetics. In addition, since hierarchy is a relational concept which logically implies the existence of an integrated universal world order, the educator who accepts such a viewpoint should emphasize the enhancement of the ability of his students to interrelate the facts that they learn into orderly wholes. This emphasis would clearly entail the utilization of essay-type examinations which consist of questions which require the student to integrate his knowledge in contrast to the generality of objective tests which stress discrete facts and understandings.

The educational counselor who accepts a hierarchical metaphysics would deem it to be one of his major functions to guide students so that they would find their proper positions in the human hierarchy, which positions would in turn be determined by their functions in society; for, as we saw earlier, the conservative hierarchical approach has been basically functional in approach. Hence, such a counselor would emphasize the importance of differential psychology and of various kinds of measurements of the students' fitness for the various roles in society. Furthermore, the counselor would be unlikely to expound sweeping universal nostrums applicable to all students. Instead, each student would presumably be evaluated in accordance with his own distinctive characteristics, to the degree that the counselor understands the nature of these characteristics.

The Concept of Natural Law

An important consequence of the conception of the universe as an orderly rational system is the advocacy of natural law, a doctrine which has played an immense role in the history of occidental thought. The advocates of natural law ground the rules of moral obligation either in human nature or in the structural characteristics of the world in which they live. There are thus various conceptions of natural law. In the past, natural law theories were propounded which were based on such diverse criteria as human reason, the moral sentiments of the individual, the conditions necessary for human survival, and the Darwinian theory of evolution. The only kind of natural law theory which has however had wide appeal for conservatives is the theory wherein natural law is grounded on the concept of universal metaphysical order. The good of each

31

thing is thus conceived in terms of the fulfillment of its function as part of a universal hierarchy. This theory contrasts sharply with other theories whereby natural law is based on the existence of single faculties and those which stress natural rights to the neglect of duties.[8]

It is today a well recognized fact that the dominant influence in the development of metaphysically based natural law theories originated with Cicero, although Plato and Aristotle had expounded similar views. Cicero's viewpoint was subsequently enlarged and made much more explicit through the writings of St. Thomas Aquinas and Richard Hooker. As thus reinterpreted, these ideas have exerted a strong influence on the thinking of more recent conservative writers like Edmund Burke and Leo Strauss. One of Cicero's most important contributions was to popularize the concept of "right reason," by which he meant reasoning in accordance with natural law for the purpose of distinguishing between right and wrong conduct. This is an essentially practical ability, although based upon metaphysical principles. In both their theory and its applications, the adherents of traditional metaphysically based natural law doctrines have implicitly recognized the importance of reason as the means of comprehending what was for them an essentially rational universe.

From the seventeenth century, metaphysical conceptions of natural law, based upon assumptions of the existence and knowability of a rationally ordered universe, have been under continuous attack by adherents of other views. During the seventeenth and the eighteenth centuries, human nature replaced the order of the universe as the primary touchstone of natural law doctrines. The stress was either on human drives as in the writings of Thomas Hobbes or on the alleged nature of early man as in the writings of John Locke and Jean Jacques Rousseau. Finally, in the nineteenth century, advocates of positive law and hedonistic utilitarianism attacked the concept of natural law itself. The deliquescence of natural law reflected the diminution of belief in metaphysical doctrines generally which has been a dominant characteristic of recent Western intellectual history. Needless to say, conservatives have consistently resisted this trend.

Implicit in the acceptance of natural law based upon a hierarchical conception of the universe is the existence of a system of values whereby the universe is ordered. These values possess ontic status because they exist independently of the mind of the observer as part of the intrinsic character of the universe. Since such an order is conceived of in objective rather than subjective terms, it is generally held to be absolute—that is to say possessed of universal validity independent of relative circumstances. The reader is referred to the discussion on the ordering of values in the first section of this chapter wherein an order of being was set forth and followed by an ordering of values in terms of their intrinsic natures rather than circumstantial accidents —all based upon the prevalent metaphysical assumptions of conservatism. Such a system of values is consistent with metaphysical natural law doctrines.

The educational implications of the conservative viewpoint on natural law are substantially similar to those entailed by the acceptance of the conservative concept of hierarchy since the latter constitutes the essential foundation of metaphysically based natural law doctrines generally. Yet the fact that conservatives believe that an entire system of moral obligation can be derived from the objective nature of the universe would lend great urgency to one of the previously noted educational consequences of conservatism—the stress upon the development in students of a comprehension of the axiological order of the universe. One of the primary problems of educational counseling and teaching from the conservative perspective pertains to the need to develop in students a comprehension of the meaning of their lives in relationship to the universal world order. This might well transcend in importance the other main function of the conservative counselor—the guidance of students toward their proper places in the human hierarchy.

The Concept of Human Nature

Conservatives are inclined to view humans as weak and imperfect creatures. Humans tend to be dominated in both their thoughts and actions by their emotions. It is only by the exercise of self-restraint that men are able to act constructively. In fact, Burke attributed most of the miseries which humans have inflicted on themselves to such attitudes and passions as "pride, ambition, avarice, revenge, lust, sedition, hypocricy, ungovern zeal" and all the other "disorderly appetites" which trouble the lives of people.[9] Both the selfishness and the emotionalism of men must be curbed by the civilizing influences of society if they are not to revert to barbarism.

When writings of the decline of chivalry, Burke exemplified this attitude in a famous quotation:
"But now all is to be changed. All the pleasing illusions which made power gentle and obedience liberal, which harmonized the different shades of life and which, by a bland assimilation, incorporated into politics the sentiments which beautify and soften private society, are to be dissolved by this conquering empire of light and reason. All the decent drapery of life is to be rudely torn off. All the superadded ideas, furnished from the wardrobe of a moral imagination, which the heart owns and the understanding ratifies as necessary to cover the defects of our naked, shivering nature and to raise it to dignity in our own estima-

34

tion, are to be exploded as a ridiculous, absurd, and anti-quated fashion."[10]

The preceding quotation contains the essence of the conservative view of human nature; for Burke viewed human problems from the perspective of one who ponders how institutions should restrain men from manifesting their intrinsic animality. The answer Burke gave was in terms of an appeal to intuitive insights as ratified by reason, for he felt that reason alone was an insufficient guide since the stock of reason in each man was limited. He especially stressed the moral imagination, a concept which was to play an important role in the thinking of Irving Babbitt and of Paul Elmer More. By imagination, Burke referred to the power of mentally reproducing the images of things and of combining them.[11] By moral imagination, he evidently meant the power of combining images in terms of moral values. In other words, he sought to view things in ethical perspective. Like many other conservatives, Burke believed that man's imagination dominated over his reason. Thus, he viewed the mind of man as not simply a *tabula rasa* at birth but rather as an active and creative instrument. This view, like so much else that Burke has espoused, presaged a dominant attitude of conservatives of both the nineteenth and twentieth centuries.

Although conservatives have been slow to recognize it, a strong linkage exists between the conservative viewpoint and the inheritance theory of human development. Specifically, the problem of how much of human variability can be attributed to nature as against nurture is one that is pregnant with political implications. It has been common practice to assert that heredity and environment are so closely intertwined that it is impossible to separate the two. Regardless of the question of the validity of this assertion, writers have tended to stress one or the other of these factors. Liberals have emphasized environmental causation since at least as far back as the time of John Locke. While the conservative position on this matter has been less clear, most of the prominent eugenicists have advocated essentially conservative views. Certainly, the inheritance theory has been more in accord with the conservative view of the rigidity of human nature than with the confidence in social reform generally characteristic of the social democratic liberals and the still greater confidence of the radicals. Furthermore, the emphasis upon heredity is more consonant with the aristocratic dimension of conservative thought than environmentalism for, once the assumption is made that the significant differences between individuals are the products of external causes, a basic obstacle is removed for the advocacy of equalitarian social policies.[12]

Although, as we have just seen, the aristocratic aspect of conservatism is congruent with a stress on biological factors in explaining human differences, it also leads to an emphasis upon the social factor as well in the sense of the orientation of people toward group life. The hierarchical ontology implicitly entails a stress upon interrelationships. The individual member of a hierarchy acquires his basic significance by standing in a certain relationship to others on the scales of being and values. Conservatives similarly regard society as a single unified structure of which they believe that one of the basic problems that the individual should solve is how to find his proper place. Hence, when conservatives discourse on politics, they are likely to view problems from the perspective of society as a whole rather than in terms of the particular needs of individual groups within the social organism.

A more specific cause of the social emphasis of conservatives was the influence of Aristotle's *Politics*. As previously noted, Aristotle's doctrines have exercised great influence upon conservative thought. Not the least of these was the Aristotelian view of society. Aristotle believed that humans were gregarious in nature and must therefore find their fulfillment as members of communities. Thus the state was deemed to be a positive good rather than a necessary evil. It was considered to be an outgrowth of the family. As such, it was conceived of as existing not simply to provide police protection but more broadly for the purpose of contributing to the virtue and well-being of its inhabitants. It is, therefore, not surprising that while individuals who are generally conservative like Burke may have been advocates of laissez-faire, the general tendency of conservatives has been to accept a fair amount of state control. The shock that some Americans have experienced in viewing the number of controls that British conservatives have been willing to accept is explicable. Most American "conservatives" are, as we have seen, classical liberals with a confidence in the self-reliance and self-sufficiency of people which is conspicuously lacking among authentic conservatives. The differences between these two groups regarding the extent and desirability of state controls is ultimately reducible to dissimilar conceptions of human nature.

Conservatives have for quite some time been disturbed over the increasing alienation of individuals from society. Three kinds of alienation have been of special concern: alienation from moral and religious values; from cultural values; and from meaningful interpersonal relationships. The sense of alienation from moral and religious values was often attributed to the growing skepticism of anything which could not be scientifically verified. The result has been the lack of a sense of direction among large numbers of people; combined with a concomitant sense of the meaninglessness of life. Concerning cultural values, Eric and Mary Josephson have expressed the situation concisely and well: "Although mass society is a political as well as a cultural phenomenon, many of its critics, among them Ortega y Gasset and T. S. Eliot, have concentrated their attack chiefly against what they regard as its vulgar values, its sameness, its threat to 'high' culture. While one may share their concern about the danger of standardized tastes, or about the threat which mass behavior in politics or in culture poses for individual expression, there is far more to the problem than this—indeed, far more than many aristocratically inclined critics of mass society (and of democracy) want to see."[13]

The Josephsons then went on to describe the atomization of society from meaningful social relationships. But they were quite wrong in their contention that the aristocratically inclined have not been aware of this situation as we shall see later.[14] The Josephsons were however essentially correct in their contention that the basis of the aristocratic opposition to mass culture was the threat posed by the latter to individual creativeness. Mass culture appeals fundamentally to a composite average. While to a certain extent it satisfies the tastes of most individuals, it does not really satisfy anyone's tastes completely. The mass media have tended to routinize culture thereby reducing its appeal to a fairly low common denominator.

The third form of alienation to arouse conservatives is the alienation of the individual from society. The most basic and ubiquitous social associations have been the family, the community, and the church. It has largely been within the confines of these institutions that individuals have sought the satisfaction of their needs for affection, friendship, and a sense of purposefulness. Yet the functions of these institutions have been gradually eroded through the expansion of huge mass institutions, especially the state. The transformations of the family exemplify the process. The educational functions have been largely taken over by the public schools; the vocational functions, by factories and offices; the entertainment that was once largely provided through the cooperation of members of the family, by television and other mass media. The problem now centers on how the family can efficiently discharge its remaining functions when so many other activities have been taken away from it. Some of these trends were unavoidable, but this does not mitigate the deleteriousness of the consequences.

The sociologist Robert A. Nisbet has probably written more extensively on the social implications of conservatism than any other conservative writer. In common with other conservatives, Nisbet believed that one of the gravest dangers confronting Western culture was the emergence of a mass of fundamentally rootless individuals, bereft of those social and cultural relationships through which humans obtain their sense of community with others and with society as a whole.[15] He attributed this consequence to a long series of historical events. The emphasis upon individualism at the time of the Reformation led to the neglect of man's social nature. Furthermore, the rise of modern capitalism, with its implicit stress upon competition rather than cooperation and upon workers as mere commodities to be bought and sold on an open market, has greatly exacerbated the trend toward the atomization of society. Since the outbreak of the French Revolution, the state has added steadily to its powers thereby undermining those intermediate associations, such as guilds and charitable associations, through which people sought companionship and a sense of unity with the social community as a whole. In common with a number of other sociologists, both conservative and non-conservative, Nisbet has attributed to the state the primary role in atomizing society; for in addition to a monopoly of force, the state has control over education, supervision over the family, power over property, and even some measure of control over personal habits. In fact, Nisbet has characterized the fundamental conflict in modern history as being not between the state and the individual but between the state and the social group.[16] The contrast be-

39

tween Nisbet's view and classical liberalism can be most clearly brought out by considering the following quotation:

"I cannot help thinking that what we need above all else in this age is a new philosophy of *laissez faire*. The old *laissez faire* failed because it was based on erroneous premises regarding human behavior. As a theory it failed because it mistook for ineradicable characteristics of individuals qualities that were in fact inseparable from social groups. As a policy it failed because its atomistic propositions were inevitably unavailing against the reality of enlarging masses of insecure individuals. Far from proving a check upon the growth of the omnicompetent state, the old *laissez faire* actually accelerated this growth. Its indifference to every form of community and association left the State as the sole area of reform and security.... To create the conditions within which the *autonomous individuals* could prosper, could be emancipated from the binding ties of kinship, class, and community, was the objective of the older *laissez faire*. To create conditions within which *autonomous groups* may prosper must be, I believe, the prime objective of the new *laissez faire*."[17] The foregoing quotation not only serves as an illustration of a concrete application of the conservative view of human nature but also highlights the fact that while conservatives generally prefer that the powers of the state extend beyond the narrow confines of law and order advocated by the classical liberals, they believe that state powers have become much too broad in scope.

The social philosophy of conservatives has been based upon a conception of human nature as insecure; lacking in both autonomy and self-sufficiency. As is well-known, such conservatives as Nisbet and Russell Kirk have viewed humans as creatures constantly beset by anxiety. Fundamental human needs were deemed to be security, status, and meaning. The first two categories, and to a partial extent the third as well, relate to needs that must be satisfied in

40

society. Neuroses are not viewed as fundamentally out-comes of early childhood experiences nor of conflicts between human emotions and repressions but rather much more frequently as the results of disturbed relations between the individual and his social environment. To conservatives, humans are not adventurous souls ready to cast asunder all the ties binding them to their companions but are rather weak beings, constantly in need of emotional reassurance. To contemporary conservatives, the most pathetic of all human types is the rootless proletarian, bereft of all the familiar ties of religion, class, and community. Marxists attribute alienation to largely economic factors; Freudians, to repressions; liberals, to social institutions; but to conservatives, the fundamental root of contemporary alienation is contained within the confines of the emotional needs of man.

It was partly because they viewed human nature as being emotionally insecure that conservatives from Edmund Burke to Russell Kirk have strongly emphasized the value and importance of tradition. In the commonly accepted meaning of the term, tradition designates the process of transmission from generation to generation of knowledge, beliefs, and attitudes as well as the products of that inheritance. To conservatives, it has more particularly signified the inherited political, moral, religious, and intellectual values of a culture that are the products of centuries of collective experience. When the irrationality and weaknesses of the individual are contrasted with the time-tested experience of the race, conservatives contend that unless the evidence is overwhelmingly to the contrary, tradition should prevail. A quotation from the writings of Edmund Burke, perhaps the most vigorous exponent of tradition, should make this position abundantly clear.

"You see, Sir, that in this enlightened age I am bold enough to confess that we are generally men of untaught feelings, that instead of casting away all our old prejudices, we cherish them to a very considerable degree, and, to take more shame to ourselves, we cherish them because they are prejudices; and the longer they have lasted and the more generally they have prevailed, the more we cherish them. We are afraid to put men to live and trade each on his own private stock of reason, because we suspect that this stock in each man is small, and that the individuals would do better to avail themselves of the general bank and capital of nations and of ages. Many of our men of speculation, instead of exploding general prejudices, employ their sagacity to discover the latent wisdom which prevails in them. If they find what they seek, and they seldom fail, they think it more wise to continue the prejudice, with the reason involved, than to cast away the coat of prejudice and to leave nothing but the naked reason; because prejudice with its reason, has a motive to give action to that reason and an affection which will give it permanence."[18]

Burke believed that traditions should be based on the long-term experience of the race communicated over countless generations; for the ultimate consequences of events seemed to him to be seldom immediately apparent. It was this attitude which prevented Burke's defense of tradition from becoming an apology for either opportunism or for whatever short-term traditions there might be which would be in the ascendent. Burke had confidence that, given sufficient time, all traditions would tend to conform to conservative standards.

"The science of constructing a commonwealth or renovating it or reforming it, is, like every other experimental science, not to be taught *a priori*. Nor is it a short experience that can instruct us in that practical science, because the real effects of moral causes are not always immediate; but that which in the first instance is prejudicial may be excellent in its remoter operation, and its excellence may arise even from the ill effects it produces in the beginning. The reverse also happens: and very plausible schemes with very pleasing commencements have often shameful and lamentable conclusions. In states there are often some obscure and almost latent causes, things which appear at first view of little moment, on which a very great part of its prosperity or adversity may most essentially depend. The science of government being therefore so practical in itself and intended for such practical purposes—a matter which requires experience and even more experience than any person can gain in his whole life, however sagacious and observing he may be—it is with infinite caution that any man ought to venture upon pulling down an edifice which has answered in any tolerable degree for ages the common purposes of society, or on building it up again without having models and patterns of approved unity before his eyes."[19]

In addition to this essentially empirical justification of tradition, a case has also been frequently made for tradition as a means for bolstering authority; for through traditional means, the values of a culture are transmitted from one generation to another. Given the conservative belief in the selfish and irrational nature of mankind, traditional processes could be considered important means whereby civilization can be protected against the excesses of unrestrained human nature. Burke has expressed this viewpoint very eloquently:

"Who would insure a tender and delicate sense of honor to beat almost with the first impulses of the heart when no man could know what would be the test of honor in a nation continually varying the standard of its coin? Nor part of life would retain its acquisitions. Barbarism with regard to science and literature, unskillfulness with regard to art and manufactures, would infallibly succeed to the want of a steady education and settled principle; and thus the commonwealth itself would, in a few generations, crumble away, be disconnected into the dust and powder of individuality, and at length dispersed to all the winds of heaven."[20] Tradition is, after all, the means whereby the moral, cultural, and religious values of mankind, accumulated through centuries of effort and experience, are communicated from generation to generation. To emphasize the value and importance of past experience is ultimately to stress the significance of history and at the same time to evince skepticism in the capacity of human reason unaided by experience to effectively order human affairs. Thus, while conservatives stress the value of metaphysical principles, in the application of these principles, they also believe in the importance of experience because of their acute consciousness of human limitations.

The educational implications of the conservative interpretation of human nature are on the whole congruent with the implications of their hierarchical conception of the universe generally. The emphasis upon heredity would, for example, lead to the same concentration upon the education of the gifted and the same stress on a variety of curricula to accord with differences in the intrinsic natures of students. Selective education, at least beyond the level needed for minimal functioning in our complex society, is a logical consequence of the emphasis on the genetic potentialities of students; for if the potentialities are inadequate, efforts to improve their performance environmentally would in the long run prove fruitless and would presumably detract from attention to the well endowed.

The conservative belief in the irrational and selfish nature of mankind clearly implies an educational approach characterized by a strong emphasis upon discipline and obedience to authority. It would hardly be wise to leave students to their own devices if they were not to be trusted. Furthermore, if one really believes in the fundamental irrationality of humans generally, it would seem to follow that the curriculum one would find acceptable would consist of required rather than elective courses, both because of a lack of confidence in the ability of people to make rational choices and of a desire to expose them to a prescribed training to enhance the rational elements of their natures. In addition, the freedom to teach students whatever one desires would hardly be promoted by adherence to an irrationalist psychology. Consistent advocates of conservatism might well be reluctant to teach anything which might undermine the morality of their students except possibly where student bodies are highly select; for the confidence that the students themselves would be able to correct any wrong impressions which the material might convey would very likely be absent.

Yet the conservative conception of education is not quite as teacher-centered as the foregoing discussion might indicate. As we have seen before, the conservative views the student as fundamentally active and creative by nature. This viewpoint is implicit in the conservative stress on the moral imagination and on the pattern of abilities which each individual student is believed to have by virtue of his heredity. To the conservative, the teacher must uphold authority and serve as a guide to the students both because of the presumably superior competence of the teacher and the need for order in the classroom. In addition, the teacher must, however, adjust his classroom procedure to take account of the individual uniqueness of each pupil. Therefore, the conservative conception of education would be neither essentially active nor passive in character but rather would properly be interactive in nature. There would therefore ideally be a constant interchange between educators and their charges.[21]

If, as conservatives believe, humans have a strong need for companionship and status among their associates, it would follow that school counselors guided by conservative values would be anxious to provide their charges with the means to satisfy these needs. This would presumably include extra-curricular social activities involving students of compatible tastes and interests. In addition, this emphasis upon the importance of man's emotional nature implies attention to the aesthetic as well as the strictly academic subjects, for it cannot be denied that one of the main purposes of aesthetic endeavor pertains to the understanding and communication of feelings. The importance of training the feelings is clearly implicit in the recognition of the paramount importance of the emotional aspect of human nature.

The advocacy of tradition as a means of overcoming some of the imperfections of human nature also involves some important educational entailments. One of the justifications offered by conservatives in the past for traditions was, as we have seen, that these represent the distilled wisdom of countless generations. By the same token, it logically follows that conservative educators would emphasize the utilization of those books and paintings which have likewise survived the test of time. In addition, attention would be given to such subjects as history and literature which consist in large part of content which reflects past experience. These subjects would presumably be taught so as to convey the moral and intellectual values which are products of past experience; for another of the major arguments used to justify traditionalism was that tradition was a superior means for the preservation and transmission of these values. It is also to be expected that in their teaching, conservatives would utilize the lives of great personages as models for imitation; because imitation was surely a major means for the transmission of traditions.

The conservative approach to the nature of man and the universe has been primarily ontological in nature, based upon an essentially hierarchical conception of being and of values. The fundamental method was to seek the rational

46

principles which determine the nature of being. Although conservatives have utilized experience as an important auxiliary determinant, their basic approach has been metaphysical. In this connection, the conservative distrust of human nature was based as much on the irrationality as on the selfishness of mankind. This attitude is the key to much of conservative educational theory; for many of the characteristics mentioned in this chapter as educational entailments of conservatism are actually means rather than ends. These consequences include the emphasis on discipline, selectivity, interaction, human differences, imitation, and other such features. The foregoing are essentially methods of increasing the efficiency of instruction. The fundamental end of conservatism, in view of the hierarchical metaphysics basic to conservative thought, is the training of potential leadership through the nurture of their powers of ratiocination so that they might intelligently discern the rational design of the universe. By this means, it is hoped that they can acquire the ability to discriminate between the noble and the petty, the refined and the vulgar, the right and the wrong, the sacred and the profane, the intelligent and the stupid—all in terms of the structural-functional pattern passed on to us from Aristotle and those whom he influenced. To put it more broadly, education from the conservative point of view is essentially a matter of understanding the nature of the universal hierarchy for the purpose of realizing the axiological significance thereof. Education would therefore ultimately be of the nature of instruction in value discrimination in accordance with the concept of a universal value hierarchy.

In this chapter, the fundamental assumptions undergirding conservative educational theory have been uncovered together with their educational entailments. In the following three chapters, historical evidence will be examined to determine the actual educational effects of the acceptance of the conservative viewpoint. If some of the consequences mentioned in this chapter are not supported by such evidence, this would not necessarily imply that the inferences made are incorrect but that quite possibly these entailments are real but unrecognized. If, on the other hand, those writers that we will study do provide us with evidence, this material should make us more certain of the generalizations made. In addition, we may thus be able to uncover some unforeseen consequences.

In the next three chapters, neo-conservative writers on education will be divided into three schools: those who have combined humanism with traditionalism; those humanists who while favorable to traditionalism have not made it a major element in their philosophies; and finally those who have had a basically religious approach to educational problems. As examples of these three schools of thought, T. S. Eliot and Russell Kirk will represent the first school; Irving Babbitt and G. H. Bantock, the second; and Bernard Iddings Bell, the third. We will begin with traditional humanism because, although Babbitt's neo-humanism may have been the first of the neo-conservative movements to appear, traditionalist humanism is the closest neo-conservative approximation to the original form of modern conservatism—the Burkean conservatism of the eighteenth century.

NOTES

[1]Aristotle, *Nicomachean Ethics* 1. 7. 1098ª.

[2]Sir Thomas Elyot, *The Book named the Governor* (London: Dent, 1962), pp. 3-4.

[3]Richard Hooker, *Of the Laws of the Ecclesiastical Polity* (London: Dent, 1907) Vol. 1, pp. 185-186, 190.

[4]See Wynne, *Theories of Education, passim.* Various value theories of the educational left, center, and right, were taken up in this book and the subjectivist axiological leanings of most left-wing educational thinkers was clearly indicated.

[5]St. Thomas ranked the virtues pertaining to the contemplation and appreciation of God separately from the natural virtues. These religious virtues were rated by their closeness to God. Aristotle did not recognize such a category of virtues.

[6]Paul Elmer More, *Aristocracy and Justice* (Boston: Houghton Mifflin Company, 1915), p. 56.

[7]*Ibid.*, p. 54.

[8]For a collection of writings on natural law by conservatives, see Robert L. Schuettinger, ed., *The Conservative Tradition in European Thought* (New York: Putnam's, 1970), pp. 117-174.

[9]Edmund Burke, *Reflections on the Revolution in France* (New York: The Liberal Arts Press, 1955), p. 162.

[10]*Ibid.*, p. 87.

[11]Burke defined imagination in his *On the Sublime and Beautiful* (New York: P. F. Collier & Son, 1937), p. 16. His was, of course, the traditional definition of the term dating back at least to the time of Aristotle.

[12]For an extended discussion of this entire question, see my paper "Genetics and Political Conservatism," *The Western Political Quarterly* 12 (September, 1959), 753-762.

[13]Eric and Mary Josephson, editors, *Man Alone* (New York: Dell Publishing Company, 1962), pp. 41-42.

[14]See especially the discussion on R. A. Nisbet in this chapter and on Russell Kirk in the next chapter.

[15]Robert A. Nisbet, *Community and Power* (New York: Oxford University Press, 1962), pp. 198-199.

[16]*Ibid.*, p. 108.

[17]*Ibid.*, p. 278.

[18]Burke, *Reflections*, pp. 98-99.

[19]*Ibid.*, pp. 69-70.

[20]*Ibid.*, p. 109.

[21]This is a logical entailment of conservative thought. We shall see later whether the thought of individual conservatives will enable us to further substantiate this generalization.

CHAPTER III

TRADITIONALIST HUMANISM: THE VIEWS OF T. S. ELIOT AND RUSSELL KIRK

Classical humanism has historically exercised a tremendous influence upon the development of Western education. As we shall see later, a large proportion of neo-conservative writers are still guided by humanistic standards in their views on educational and cultural issues. It is therefore important to understand the meaning of humanism as a doctrine or viewpoint. This will be accomplished by focusing on those characteristics which the various classical humanistic movements of the past had in common.

The ultimate aim of the classical humanists was the improvement of the individual person.[1] Instead of seeking the collective elevation of humanity, the humanists preferred to work on an individual basis. In general, humanists did not believe that humans were completely perfectible, but they had confidence in the improvability of mankind.

The means that humanists advocated for attaining the goal of individual improvement were predicated on the concept of harmony. By harmony, they had reference to the ideal of the perfect articulation and integration of characteristics to produce an agreeable whole. This involved a combination of symmetry, balance, and proportion. As such, it was fundamentally an aesthetic ideal. Humanists stressed the value of literature and the fine arts for, among other reasons, the development of a sense of harmony. More broadly, harmony as an educational ideal implied the development of the versatile individual in whom the various academic and personal excellences would be blended into a decorous whole whereby excesses would be avoided and an approach made to the Aristotelian doctrine of the mean, the ethical expression of harmony.[2]

Historically, the humanistic viewpoint developed in ancient Greece. Such Greek and Roman writers as Plato, Aristotle, Isocrates, Cicero, and Quintilian laid the foundations of the movement. Humanism was also an important influence during the Renaissance. In addition, classical humanism influenced the development of the traditional liberal arts education of Europe and America. Contemporary humanism can be divided into two schools: one which is elitist in nature; the other of a more democratic orientation.[3] The more democratic school is exemplified by the writings of Mark Van Doren, Gilbert Highet, and Jacques Barzun.[4] This school of thought is obviously not conservative in any discriminating sense of the term due to the absence of the aristocratic dimension of conservatism. It is therefore elitist humanism that will command our attention.

Those neo-conservatives with a humanistic approach to education can be divided into two groups. One group combined humanism with the espousal of cultural traditionalism. The second group, while not unfavorable to traditionalism, has not evinced the same degree of confidence in it. Instead, the members of this second group have preferred to state their position in more modernistic terms. The most influential neo-conservative writers on education to expound a traditionalist version of humanism were T. S.

Eliot and Russell Kirk; their more modernistically inclined counterparts were Irving Babbitt and G. H. Bantock. This chapter will be devoted to the traditional humanists; the following to the more modernist group.

The approach of the traditionalistic humanists was both socio-cultural and aesthetic since they were concerned with preserving the values of their culture and their society—especially pertaining to the traditional ways of living of the people. In addition, they were concerned with the importance of culture in another sense of the term—aesthetic and intellectual cultivation. A prime example of this combination is T. S. Eliot.

The Work of T. S. Eliot

Eliot had the rather uncommon distinction of being one of the seminal influences of the twentieth century in at least two lines of endeavor—poetry and cultural criticism. It is as a cultural critic that he will be of concern to us for the influence that he had exerted on conservative thought stemmed primarily from his role as a critic of the times.

Eliot was born in St. Louis, Missouri, on September 26, 1888, the scion of a prominent family. His grandfather, a Unitarian minister, was a founder and subsequently chancellor of the George Washington University of St. Louis. Eliot's father was president of a brick manufacturing company and a patron of the arts. The poet's mother, Charlotte Champe Stearns Eliot, was a poetess herself. It can be assumed that T. S. Eliot had, as a child, the inestimable advantage of growing up in a highly cultivated household.

Eliot received a traditional classical education in the preparatory department of Washington University and subsequently at Milton Academy. He entered Harvard in 1906 where he concentrated largely on literature and on philosophy. Eliot graduated Harvard in 1909 and received the Master of Arts degree in English literature from the same institution in 1910. Before returning to Harvard for further study, Eliot spent a delightful year in Paris studying French literature and philosophy. He then began working toward the Ph.D. degree at Harvard University, changing his major field. Partially under the influence of one of his Harvard professors, Irving Babbitt, Eliot enrolled in Indic studies but later switched to philosophy. The poet did not complete the requirements for the doctorate since other concerns overshadowed his academic plans. He did complete his dissertation which pertained to a conservatively inclined philosopher, F. H. Bradley. Eliot planned to present his dissertation to his committee but, at the time that his thesis was completed, he was living in England and missed the boat back to the United States. One cannot help wondering why he did not board another ship. In any case, it was evident that by this time some very fundamental changes had occurred in Eliot's way of life.

In 1914, Eliot went to England to study philosophy at Oxford, presumably in connection with his dissertation on F. H. Bradley. He evidently decided to remain in England. In 1915, he married Vivienne Haigh-Wood of London and became a schoolteacher. Eliot first taught at High Wycombe and later at Highgate Junior School in London. He found teaching to be very strenuous and especially disliked the task of maintaining discipline. He left teaching for a position in the Foreign and Colonial Department at Lloyd's Bank while working during evenings and weekends on his poetry. In 1925, Eliot met Geoffrey Faber, who was interested in hiring a writer with a reputation who could attract young writers to work for Faber's publishing company. Eliot eventually became a director of Faber and Faber and utilized his position to encourage individuals with strong poetic talents. In 1948, Eliot was awarded the Nobel prize in literature. In 1957, long after the death of his first wife, Eliot married his secretary, Valerie Fletcher. He found the happiness in his second marriage which had eluded him during his first marriage. Eliot died in London on January 4, 1965. As is well-known, Eliot announced his conversion from the Unitarian to the Anglo-Catholic faith in 1928. At the same time, he proclaimed himself a classicist in literature and a royalist in politics.

Eliot was primarily a philosophical poet. His two most influential poems were probably *The Waste Land* (1922) and *Ash Wednesday* (1930). The earlier poem dealt with the spiritual aridity of the twentieth century; the later poem with the Christian answer to the problems of the age. Both of these poems were highly abstract and symbolic in nature and helped to stimulate revolutionary changes in twentieth-century poetry.

During the latter half of his life, Eliot evinced a considerable concern about sociological and cultural problems. His most influential work in this area was *Notes Towards the Definition of Culture* (1949) which examined the meanings of the term "culture" and the conditions needed for cultural creativity. Only slightly less influential was *The Idea of a Christian Society* (1940) in which he dealt with what he believed to be the desirable structure and aims of a society based upon Christian values. Although other works will be utilized in our examintion of Eliot's social and cultural thought, these two works probably contain a greater volume of relevant material than any of Eliot's other publications; so that our analysis will be based largely on these materials.

While we can certainly speculate on the nature of the influences upon Eliot, it is safer to rely on his own testimony as to the persons who influenced him in the writing of these two important works. In the writing of the *Notes*, Eliot has indicated that he was influenced primarily by the writings of Canon V. A. Demant, Christopher Dawson, Karl Mannheim, and Dwight McDonald.[5] Canon Demant and Christopher Dawson were well-known writers on the social implications of religious thought. Karl Mannheim was of course the famous sociologist whose views on the roles of elite and class were of particular importance to Eliot. Dwight McDonald is known primarily as a critic of mass culture. Among those who influenced Eliot concerning his views in *The Idea of a Christian Society* were Canon Demant, Dawson, Middleton Murry, and Jacques Maritain.[6] Both Murry and Maritain were vigorous advocates of social reconstruction based upon Christian principles, In general, most of the writers who influenced Eliot as a social and cultural critic were either Roman Catholic, Anglican, or secularist writers with aristocratic tendencies. Curiously, Eliot did not mention his former teacher, Irving Babbitt, with whom he shared many opinions.

The central concept of Eliot's entire social theory is "culture" which is considerably broader in scope than the political context of much existing social theory. Culture is also a more fundamental concept than "society" which is based upon culture rather than the reverse. It is therefore of considerable importance to inquire into Eliot's meaning and use of the term "culture."

To begin with, Eliot veered back and forth between two general meanings of culture. One meaning pertained to the general way of life of a people. The following is an example of this usage:

"Taking now the point of view of identification, the reader must remind himself, as the author has constantly to do, of how much is here embraced by the term culture. It includes all the characteristic activities and interests of a people: Derby Day, Henley Regetta, Cowes, the twelfth of August, a cup final, the dog races, the pin table, the dart board, Wensleydale cheese, boiled cabbage cut into sections, beetroot in vinegar, nineteenth century Gothic churches and the music of Elgar. The reader can make his own list."[7]

In addition, Eliot also sometimes equated culture with aesthetic and intellectual cultivation. In the following quotation, he gave a detailed account of the meaning of this usage of culture.

"There are several kinds of attainment which we may have in mind in different contexts. We may be thinking of refinement of manners—of urbanity and civility: if so, we shall think first of a social class, and of the superior individual as representative of the best of that class. We may be thinking of learning and a close acquaintance with the accumulated wisdom of the past: if so our man is the scholar. We may be thinking of philosophy in the widest sense—an interest in and some ability to manipulate abstract ideas. If so, we may mean the intellectual (recognizing the fact that this term is now used very loosely, to comprehend many persons not conspicuous for strength of intellect). Or we may be thinking of the arts: if so, we mean the artist and the amateur or dilettante. But what we seldom have in mind is all of these things at the same time."[8]

Eliot reconciled the two meanings of the term culture, as a general way of life and as cultivation, by viewing them as different aspects of one phenomenon. Cultivation pertained to the culture of the individual and to some extent of the group or class. However, the culture of the individual and the culture of the class both reflect the general way of life or, put another way, the culture of the whole society. Realizing this, Eliot was critical of Matthew Arnold for giving attention in *Culture and Anarchy* to the individual and class aspects of culture to the neglect of the societal aspect. Thus, Eliot exhibited the emphasis on the group which has been characteristic of conservative thinkers compared to the stress on the individual of the classical liberals.

In addition to defining the meaning of culture, Eliot also wanted to describe the conditions essential for maximum cultural productivity. He believed that there were at least three such conditions: the existence of social classes, cultural regionalism, and a balance between unity and diversity in religion.[9] Ultimately, he assumed, by naming these particular conditions, the paramount importance of balance in stimulating intellectual and aesthetic achievement. By balance, Eliot had in mind combinations of unity with diversity and of harmony with dissonance. The following discussion is designed to explain this viewpoint.

To Eliot, each social class represented a distinct way of life. In fact, he believed that the chief function of each class should be that of passing on its way of life strengthened and revitalized to future generations. The primary agency for transmitting this heritage was the family, which Eliot believed to be more important than the school as an agency of cultural transmission. An especially vital function of the family was the preservation of a standard of civility and manners.[10]

When intellectuals such as Karl Mannheim advocated the dominance of elites of talents and abilities, Eliot felt that they overlooked the equally vital role of social classes since the cultural heritage consisted of much more than facts and techniques. Instead, Eliot favored a combination of elites and social classes arranged in hierarchical patterns. In describing this hierarchy, Eliot wrote:
"What I have advanced is not a 'defense of aristocracy'—an emphasis upon the importance of one organ of society. Rather it is a plea on behalf of a form of society in which there will be, from 'top' to 'bottom,' a continuous gradation of cultural levels: it is important to remember that we should not consider the upper levels as possessing more culture than the lower, but as representing a more conscious culture and a greater specialization of culture. I

incline to believe that no true democracy can maintain itself unless it maintains these different levels of culture."[11]

Eliot believed that a people should be neither too united nor too divided if culture is to flourish. Either extreme could lead to tyranny. On the one hand, a graded social hierarchy is desirable. On the other hand, members of different classes should possess a community of common culture which would enable them to mix freely. In other words, classes should exist but should not become rigidly stratified into castes.[12]

Eliot also favored the encouragement and preservation of local regional cultures since he believed that cultural diversity enriches the cultures of the world. On the one hand, cultures need to attract each other to affect one another; on the other hand, a certain degree of repulsion is also needed for particular cultures to survive. An example of what he desired is the "satellite culture." He felt that this was well exemplified by the cultures of the Irish, the Scots, and the Welsh which he regarded as satellites of the allegedly more dominant English culture. As satellites, these cultures have greatly enriched English culture and, by the same token, have played a greater role in the world than would have been true had they preserved their cultural independence. By using the English language, Irish, Welsh, and Scottish writers have reached a larger audience than if they had written in the languages which once were their native vernaculars. The range of thought and feeling represented in English literature has been enlarged not only because these writers used English, but also because these writers have expressed and reflected the distinctive characteristics of their native cultures. To reduce all the cultures of Great Britain to one would have limited the range of literary achievement.[13]

The same combination of unity and diversity was characteristic of the poet's view of the relationship of religion to culture. He felt that those religions were most culturally stimulating which were capable of winning acceptance by people from widely diverse cultures. Such religions provided a pattern of common belief which encourages cultural interchanges between peoples. On the other side, religious diversity was needed to avoid petrification which would lead to either torpor or chaos, depending on the natures of the peoples affected. In fact, Eliot feared that a reunion of the Christian churches would result in a lowering of the general cultural level through the lessening of religious diversity.[14]

A continual struggle between the centripetal and the centrifugal forces of religious unity and diversity was deemed to be highly desirable for without such a struggle, balance could not be maintained. Christianity should be one but, within it, there should be an endless conflict of ideas; for truth is clarified and enlarged through intellectual struggle.[15]

Eliot's emphasis upon diversity was, as we have seen, consistent with the general direction of conservative thought.[16] He had, however, confidence in the eventual triumph of truth through discussion and struggle which far exceeded what was usual among conservatives. The conservative view of the irrationality of man would tend to mitigate such confidence. In this respect, Eliot was somewhat more hopeful than his spiritual allies.

Eliot's love of diversity obviously implied the cultivation of cultural diversities in the schools. Freedom of discussion was also clearly entailed, for rigorous censorship undermines diversity by restricting the range of views to which the individual can be exposed. The emphasis upon the retention and encouragement of a class-differentiated society also implies a multitrack system of education with different kinds of education available to individuals of diverse social backgrounds; for the advocacy of a variety of social classes implies differences in functions between these classes which entails the need for different kinds of training to fulfill these functions.

To Eliot, social issues were clearly subordinate to cultural questions. He distinguished between societies on the basis of the cultural ideals which they exemplified. On this basis, three kinds of society were distinguished. The Christian society was the type of society where behavior was regulated in accordance with Christian ideals.[17] The pagan society was described in terms antithetical to Christian ideals. While Eliot was vague concerning the attitudes inculcated by pagan societies, he cited the fascist regimes as examples.[18]

The third type of society was the one in which Eliot thought that he was living—the negative society. This type of society was not guided by an ideal unless one thought liberalism an ideal. He felt liberalism to be a movement defined by its starting point more than by ends. Eliot believed that liberalism constituted a trend away from rather than toward something definite.[19] What he probably meant was that liberalism was fundamentally the emphasis upon freedom, which was in itself not really an end but rather a means to an end. Eliot made no attempt to explain his assertion but our interpretation seems to be the only meaningful one; for, as generally interpreted, freedom signifies the absence of restraints against individual and group activities but not what should be the goals of these activities.

Eliot felt that the inefficiency of liberal society would lead to its eventual disappearance and replacement by a society that would be either Christian or pagan. Eliot commented on the malaise of liberalism: "By destroying the traditional social habits of the people, by dissolving their natural collective consciousness into individual constituents, by licensing the opinions of the most foolish, by substituting instruction for education, by encouraging cleverness rather than wisdom, the upstart rather than the qualified, by fostering a notion of getting on to which the alternative is a hopeless apathy, Liberalism can prepare the way for that which is its own negation: the artificial, mechanized, or brutalized control which is a desperate remedy for its chaos."[20]

Evidently Eliot viewed liberalism as a movement characterized by equalitarianism, an excessive emphasis upon freedom, and a hopeless absence of standards. Unless replaced by a Christian standard of values, Liberalism would lead to tyranny. In the presentation of his views on the Christian society, Eliot neglected to specify the means of bringing this society into existence nor even of defending it. He wanted to show how it would differ from the negative, liberal society in which he lived.[21] Of special concern to him was its "idea" or ends.

The aims of a Christian society would be the virtue and well-being of the people and the attainment of beatitude for those who would be capable of it.[22] A Christian society would be composed of two elements: the masses and the elite "Community of Christians." The Community of Christians would consist of those clergy and laity who are sufficiently developed spiritually and intellectually to understand Christian doctrines and to live consciously by them.[23] As for the masses, their adherence to Christianity would be behavioral and would be expressed both in their actions toward their neighbors and in customary religious observances. Eliot believed that the masses had only a minimal capacity for reflecting on the objects of faith. Instead of attempting to inculcate an understanding among them of the most abstract concerns of theology, it was far more important to convey to them a realization of how far they fell short of the Christian ideal.[24] This position implied that beyond a certain minimal level of attainment formal education should be selective in applicability. If differences in intellectual understanding were, as Eliot apparently assumed, largely due to differences in innate potentialities, there was little use in seeking to train people beyond the limits of their abilities.

Eliot believed that a nation's educational system was more important than its government. In attempting to delineate the outline of his Christian society, Eliot devoted some attention to schooling as a means of helping to bring about the smooth functioning of that society. The primary aim of schooling in this society would be to teach people to think in Christian categories, which presumably meant in terms of Christian values. Eliot considered such Christian thought to be more important than the encouragement of the outward manifestations of Christian piety, which was not necessarily a reliable indicator of the possession of Christian faith. The beliefs of the rulers of a nation were, to Eliot, of less significance than the beliefs of the population over which they ruled since the practical necessities of political life necessitated their conformity to the ideals of the citizenry of their country.[25]

Eliot believed it to be essential that there exist a certain cultural uniformity based upon agreement concerning what everyone should know. This uniformity was considered necessary to provide cultural continuity and to promote communication. In a Christian society, the content of education would in large part be determined by Christian principles. In the United States, according to Eliot, there was such pervasive permissiveness that one could not assume that any two undergraduates had read the same books or taken the same courses unless they had attended the same school and had studied with the same teacher at the same time. To Eliot, education differed from instruction in that there was some principle of selection of the knowledge which any educated person should possess. In a negative society, the ideal of wisdom was displaced by uncontrolled experimentation and permissiveness.[26] In his opposition to the elective system of education, Eliot typified conservative opinion. The conservative assumption of the existence of a natural hierarchy of value clearly implies the existence of a hierarchy of subjects which embody these values. It follows that the selection of subjects to be studied should be based on this hierarchy rather than on the personal desires of the students involved. Eliot did not make clear his reasons for opposing the elective system, but his stand is consistent with his general educational position.

As to his views concerning education in the democratic, secularist society in which he found himself, Eliot assumed a different approach; for he was confronted by a different set of questions. In general, Eliot was critical of C. E. M. Joad's statement of the purposes of education. Joad felt that education should prepare people to earn a livelihood, to become good citizens, and to develop all their latent powers.[27] Eliot felt that Joad had overlooked the value of education for its own sake—as a means for the acquisition of knowledge and wisdom as well as an appreciation of the importance of learning. Another important purpose of education should be "to preserve the class and select the elite."[28] While a particular program was not specified for achieving this goal, we can extrapolate from Eliot's general approach. Education was to be a means whereby the cultures of the various classes would be transmitted to future generations. It would also function as a means of elite selection. In an article on Eliot's viewpoint in education, Robert M. Hutchins expressed the opinion that the existence of class and elite were irrelevant to human improvement because the membership of social classes could be both wicked and stupid while members of elite groups could be wicked but apparently not stupid.[29] For his position to have much cogency, Hutchins would have to show why men would not be more wicked or more stupid without classes or elites. To argue convincingly against the encouragement of classes and elites, one would have to prove that they do at least as much harm as good. To say that classes and elites have not attained perfection is not equivalent to a denial that they do some good. Eliot did not maintain that classes and elites would make men perfect. In fact, Eliot wanted to improve classes and elites by appropriate educational reforms. He would probably view Hutchin's strictures as indicative of the need of improving the education o members of social classes and elites—not for ignoring these groups.

In any case, Eliot wished to diminish the occurrence of both wickedness and stupidity. In addition to the function assigned to education with respect to class and elite, Eliot believed in the importance of schooling as an agency both for cultural continuity and the development of the moral and intellectual faculties of mankind. In fact, he considered cultural continuity to be a major factor in the elevation of those faculties. The subjects which Eliot believed to be of special value in fostering cultural continuity were history and foreign languages.[30] Among the languages, Eliot believed that Latin and Greek were of special importance; for much of the Western Christian heritage was originally communicated through these languages.[31] In essence, Eliot sought to justify traditional humanistic education.

Like most other conservative writers on education, Eliot believed that general education was more important than vocational training. Before one can become a good citizen, one must learn how to be a good man.[32] Learning should be primarily for the purpose of acquiring wisdom. Other considerations should be secondary.[33] Even when pursuing other purposes, it was vital that students concentrated on the strictly academic subjects. For example, to become a good citizen, Eliot recommended that students should learn history, economics, and government. The value of history was not conceived in terms of familiarity with the technical aspects of government but rather as a means of developing ethical consciousness and critical thinking.[34]

Eliot was especially concerned with what he regarded as the headlong rush to educate everybody. Mass education would, he feared, lead inevitably to the lowering of academic standards and to the neglect of those subjects through which the essence of culture has been transmitted.[35] Presumably, these consequences would result from the pressure to simplify education to bring it within the reach of the masses. The poet believed that educating students above the level of their abilities would be disastrous by creating much discontent and mental strain.[36] In answer to Eliot, Hutchins denied that men could have too much education; for if wisdom is a major aim of education, who could question the view that men should have as much wisdom as possible?[37] The obvious reply from Eliot's point of view would be that if a man is not capable of understanding the educational material meted out to him, then he would be getting too much education for his abilities. Ultimately the contrast in this instance between Eliot and Hutchins is based on a wide difference of opinion pertaining to the educational potentialities of the masses. This difference might well be based upon a difference in emphasis pertaining to the relative efficacy of environment as against heredity. Unfortunately, Hutchins was not very explicit in presenting his views so that it is difficult to untangle his assumptions. Also, Eliot might have been more explicit as well.

Considerable attention was devoted by Eliot to the "equality of education" argument which he believed to be based upon three erroneous assumptions: (1) superiority is always superiority of intellect; (2) there exists an infallible means of recognizing intellect; (3) it is possible to devise a system that would infallibly nourish intellect. From these false assumptions, there has arisen the ideal of an educa-

66

tional system that would sort out everyone according to his intellectual abilities.[38]

Eliot's usage of the concept of equality of opportunity is more applicable to British than to American conditions. During the twentieth century, especially since World War II, there has been a concerted effort to replace Britain's class system of education by a meritocracy. The trend was justified in the name of "equality of opportunity." Until the last few decades, equality of opportunity had the same connotations in the United States as in Great Britain. It commonly signified the opportunity of the poor and disadvantaged individual to rise in the social and occupational hierarchy through a combination of energy, ability, and character. The stress was upon opportunity rather than equality although no such concerted effort was made to put it into effect as in present-day Britain. Today, the stress in the United States is upon equality including the utilization of racial, sex, and ethnic quota systems and on the relaxing of educational standards. This would probably have alarmed Eliot more than the British usage; for equalitarianism is obviously more antithetical to conservatism than meritocracy. The conservative stress on hierarchy is in direct opposition to the current American trend. The different attitudes toward opportunity is one of many possible illustrations of the fact that despite the alleged socialism of the British economic system, its educational system is more conservative than the American counterpart.

Although Eliot thought that the exceptional individual should have the opportunity to rise in the social scale, the aim of sorting out everyone in accordance with his or her abilities was unattainable and would disorganize society by the substitution of elites of intellect for classes. He believed that tests were not necessarily accurate indicators of the most important abilities. Rigid conformity to the educational system might actually be the real criterion of selection instead of intellectual ability. The education of everyone capable of receiving a higher education must, he thought, lead inevitably to a lowering of academic standards through the concomitant overcrowding of the schools. Mass education would also enlarge the powers of the state since it would acquire control over the means of selection which control would ultimately lead to making the ends of the state the most important consideration in higher education. Eliot believed that education could function best when there existed some balance between privilege and opportunity.[39]

Eliot's fear of overcrowding as a consequence of providing higher education for all those capable of receiving it was apparently based upon the assumption that admission standards would be sufficiently generous so that massive enrollment would be an inevitable outcome. This does not, however, necessarily follow. Standards might be set at a sufficiently high level to avoid that outcome. Perhaps Eliot thought that political pressures would militate against raising standards, but the truth of this assumption would depend on the degree of political supervision over the agencies that would regulate academic admissions standards. In any case, the level at which individuals are deemed to be capable of profiting from a university education is to some degree relative to standards of judgment so some leeway is possible.

To grasp the significance of Eliot's viewpoints, it is important to view his philosophy from a broad perspective. He was, as we have seen, reacting primarily against two contemporary trends. One of these was the decline of Christian influences together with the rise of the negative society, bereft of dedication to either religious or moral values. The other was the pressure to lower academic standards. He believed the latter trend to be the fruit of pressures both from the equalitarians and the advocates of an educational meritocracy.

His reaction to these trends was largely the consequence of his belief in the importance of cultural creativity and of religious faith. The negative society would undermine creativity by destroying the traditional social habits of the people and by undermining the class structure of society. Mass education would undermine cultural creativity by instilling pressures to lower academic standards and to neglect those subjects most important for cultural creativity. Eliot feared that the rampant moral and religious skepticism of the negative society would lead to the growth of an aggressively pagan society.

To Eliot, education was primarily an instrument for the transmission and improvement of culture. One of the major aims of education was cultural transmission; for cultural creativeness would decline if the various cultures of the world were to lose their individuality. Another of its aims, wisdom, pertained to the transmission of the insights of the past. This aim could be subsumed under the rubric of cultural transmission; for Eliot conceived of culture in such a way as to merge anthropological and aesthetic usages. In addition, Eliot was concerned with education as an instrument for training in citizenship and for class and elite recruitment. This latter function was likewise an expression of Eliot's essentially cultural anthropological approach to education; for if society is conceived of as a single cultural organism, it is important to provide for an elite to direct that society.

The Views of Russell Kirk

One of the most influential neo-conservatives is Russell A. Kirk, who has been a prolific writer of works on conservatism and was one of the founders of both *Modern Age* and the *National Review*, perhaps the two most prominent American journals of a specifically conservative slanting. Professor Kirk is a graduate of Michigan State University (1940). He subsequently received the M. A. degree from Duke University (1941) and the doctorate from St. Andrews University in Scotland (1952). From 1946 until 1953, he taught history of civilization at Michigan State. From 1957 to 1969, he was Research Professor of Politics at C. W. Post College. During the same period, he was University Professor at Long Island University. He writes and lectures extensively and makes his home, as befits a true conservative, at the domicile of his ancestors, Mecosta, Michigan. To judge by the academic posts he has occupied, Kirk's chief academic interests are apparently history and political science.

His best known works are probably *The Conservative Mind* (1953), *A Program for Conservatives* (1954), *Academic Freedom* (1955) and *Eliot and His Age* (1971). *The Conservative Mind* is a history of Anglo-American thought on conservatism from Burke to Santayana which, in the revised edition, was extended to include Eliot.[40] In his *Program*, Kirk showed how conservative principles can be applied to the social, educational, and political problems which concern us. The title *Academic Freedom* is self-explanatory. *Eliot and His Age* is devoted to the life of T. S. Eliot and to the people and ideas which influenced Eliot. As a writer, Kirk is undoubtedly an accomplished literary artist, although quite neglectful of the systematic and sustained argumentation characteristic of the skilled philosopher. As is well-known, Kirk derived the essentials of his conservative viewpoint largely from the writings of Edmund Burke.[41]

In what is perhaps the most explicit statement of Kirk's general philosophy, *A Program for Conservatives*, Kirk has named what he considered to be the ten most crucial problems which should concern the people of the United States. As will soon be evident, these are long-term problems, not evanescent in character, and were stated in Burkean terms. In viewing these questions, we can obtain a clear understanding of the nature of the Burkean approach to contemporary American problems.

The problem of the heart is one of these. Specifically, Kirk meant the question of how to enable the will to again act in accordance with ethical and spiritual precepts.[42] By "spiritual," he was evidently referring to religion; for his prescription involved both the restoration of belief in intrinsic moral values and in religious faith. The basic reason for the existence of the problem of the heart was deemed to be the decline of tradition. The fundamental criterion and source of values was considered to be the universal order of nature, established by a means "more than human."[43] Kirk had in effect grounded rightness of will on the natural law doctrine of "right reason"—obedience to the values derived from a nature conceived to be rationally ordered and therefore understandable by reason. In essence, this view implied the subordination of will to reason.

The spread of boredom among the masses constituted another of Kirk's problems. The causes for this situation were multiple. The decline of religion undermined the faith of the people in meaningful purposes and ends. The problem was exacerbated by industrialization which led to a wide-spread intoxication with machinery and to an insatiable desire for sensations. Add to these factors the undermining of individual and family responsibilities by the steady extension of the powers of the state, and the individual was thereby condemned to an empty and rudderless existence.[44]

Kirk had little confidence in the ability of the masses to find satisfactory substitutes for religious faith and a sense of individual responsibility. His remedies were tied to the

71

causes stipulated. Religion must be revived and individual self-reliance must be restored if existence is to recover its significance. Through religion, the individual would acquire the sense of purpose needed to make life meaningful, while the experience obtained through the exercise of individual responsibility would add to life's meaning.[45] To Kirk, the primary exemplification of boredom was the rootless man, bereft of both traditional supports and enduring convictions.

Boredom was closely linked to the problem of the decline of community spirit; the loss of the feeling of identity with the groups to which one belongs. The communal spirit was praised both for the sense of personal security and comradeship which it encouraged and because of the relatively unselfish striving for the common good which was a consequence. Causes for the decline of communal spirit were, according to Kirk, the gradual subversion of the autonomy of local groups by the diffusion of the powers of the state and the modern overvaluation of economic factors in contributing to or detracting from human contentment. The revival of autonomous groups and institutions were recommended together with encouragement of private schooling, thereby contributing to variety and independence in education.[46]

Several implicit assumptions underlie Kirk's position. An obvious one was that humans find their happiness in groups. For communal loyalties to be meaningful, they must be focused on local groups rather than on abstract concepts such as "humanity" or "world peace." Kirk was keenly aware of the limitations of human nature, not the least of which was the need for emotional security.

When we turn to Kirk's discussion of the problem of social justice, we are confronted with a different kind of question. The model for social justice was deemed to be a

72

hierarchical society in which each person would be found in the place best suited to his nature. The chief obstacle to social justice was believed to be rooted in the widespread resentment of excellence which Kirk considered to be a menace to both culture and society.[47] Thus, in dealing with social justice, Kirk was concerned primarily with differentiation in contrast to the stress on identity implicit in his concept of community. The ideal society must therefore possess the right balance between identity and differentiation. In the proper contexts, both factors were important.

Kirk's view of social justice contrasts with the view that equates social justice with equality. The contrasts can be stated in terms of greatly divergent conceptions of human nature and of human welfare. For the conservative, men are innately unequal. For the equalitarian, men should be considered equal in at least the most important aspects of their nature. For the conservative, the uplift of the most able is most important for progress, but for the equalitarian, it is the uplift of the masses. The conservative educator is therefore strongly inclined to concentrate on developing the talents of his most gifted students; the more equalitarian, on raising the average level of his class.

To Kirk, the fundamental cause of the pervasiveness of the resentment against excellence was the increasing dominance of the mass mind and the consequent pandering of the purveyors of culture to mediocrity. He also indicted the universities for subordinating liberal learning to the aims of utility and of sociability. To achieve social justice, in Kirk's sense of the term, there must, he thought, be an elevation of the standards of achievement.[48] Kirk's prescription seems, to this writer, to be grossly inadequate. If resentment against excellence is to be reduced, a respect for excellence must be created. This would involve an inculcation of a sense of qualitative excellence through an emphasis upon

73

developing the tastes of young people, both in the schools and in their homes.

The problem of wants is closely related to that of social justice. Specifically, the problem is how to enable people to *want* the right things from the standpoint of justice. The excessive stress on material wants to the neglect of spiritual needs implicitly involves the problems of excellence and of the inversion of values. By spiritual values, Kirk meant moral values and the ideal of qualitative excellence. His remedies included a revival of such traditional goods as justice, mercy, honor, charity, and fine craftsmanship. Decentralized industry was believed to be an important means of stimulating more people to engage in creative and responsible activity.[49]

The next problem to engage Kirk's attention, that of order, is just barely distinguishable from that of social justice, for both pertain to the concept of hierarchy. Social justice, as conceived by Kirk, pertained to the attainment of an ideal condition in which each individual would occupy the place proper to his nature. Order, as such, referred to the harmony and balance which were believed to be consequences of the attainment of social justice. Kirk believed that the harmonious arrangement of functions and ideals would guard justice. He did not directly explain the connection between harmony and justice, but he presumably meant that the spirit of harmony would produce the tranquility which would limit the development and exercise of envy. The decay of order was attributed to the decline of the spirit of community which was essential to developing social harmony since identification with the social good presumably lessens individual presumption.[50] The cure was obviously implicit in the cause—the revival of community by application of the suggestions previously made.[51]

The decline in social order was, according to Kirk, paralleled by a similar decline in the sense of order between the

74

various subjects offered in the curricula of educational institutions—especially those concerned with higher education. According to Kirk, most university administrators have accepted the view that all studies were of equal value. For example, a class in fly-casting might be considered as equal in value to one in Greek. A consequence has been a shift in emphasis from the thorough mastery of a few subjects to a superficial acquaintance with many. Kirk's own rating of the fields of study will be discussed after an analysis of his general views on education.[52]

Kirk viewed the problem of power in terms of the restraint of might by "right reason." As a concept, power had, to Kirk, negative implications; for it denoted the absence of restrictions on arbitrary human actions, and his primary concern was with limiting power out of solicitude for the preservation of traditional moral values. He also justified the restriction of power by pointing to the rise of the dictators and the two world wars as political and military consequences of the arbitrary human actions of the past. The remedy prescribed was to limit and decentralize power, although one might well wonder how the holders of power could be persuaded to part with some of that precious commodity.[53]

Perhaps part of the answer can be found in Kirk's discussion of the next problem which pertained to loyalty. The decline of loyalty to the nation and to the family was attributed to a combination of factors such as the decline of faith in religious and moral values, the general neglect of liberal education, the rise of the "gutter" press (Kirk did not explain what he meant by that), and the rise of equalitarianism. Our chief concern in this regard is with Kirk's strictures on schools and the press since newspapers are obviously educational agencies. The decline of liberal education helped to undermine loyalty since with it came a neglect of history, especially the history of one's own country. Concurrently, the literature enshrining loyalty to family and nation, such as moralistic writings and biographies of respected national figures, was also neglected. Regarding the press, Kirk may have had reference to the critical attitudes of many journalists toward traditional American values. In any case, his use of the term "gutter" indicates a strong emotional reaction. Kirk's suggestions for the revival of loyalty included the increased teaching and study of history and a greater stress upon religious values. Furthermore, Kirk would prefer to see a nation of people characterized by civility of manners, a political system where justice is fairly administered, and safe conditions so that citizens are secure against criminals. It is difficult to love a nation whose people are not lovable. Therefore, the need to elevate the manners of the people can be as pressing as the need to obtain inspiration from the American past.[54]

One of the primary problems mentioned by Kirk pertained to the need for the revival of tradition. The need was justified on several grounds. Like Burke, Kirk maintained that the principal source of our social wisdom was the experience of the race as forged through triumph and tragedy over thousands of years. Tradition was deemed to be far superior to the wisdom that any one human being could accumulate on his own; for it involved the accumulated experiences of untold numbers of people in diverse situations, confronting a fantastic range of problems. Furthermore, our moral values have traditional roots, and Kirk was convinced that these values could be much more effectively communicated through such traditional institutions as the family and the church than through formal classroom instruction. Although traditions were deemed to be in need of periodic revisions, Kirk warned that these revisions should not be undertaken heedlessly or too boldly. The presumption must always be in favor of tradition unless the case to the contrary is overwhelming.

Implicit in this position is a distrust of the sole or predominant reliance upon abstract reason in the apprehension and solution of human problems. Educationally, this distrust of the exclusive reliance on reason would encourage the non-intellectual aspects of human nature—such as the aesthetic and the experiential—not to replace the intellectual but to add to it. It also implies an emphasis upon those fields of study which can serve as vehicles for tradition—such as religion, history, and literature. To Kirk, the methods of the more abstract and intellectualized studies were not universally applicable. For him, there was no universal model of general applicability. Epistemology was in truth a multifaceted study.[55]

Lastly, we come to the problem of the mind, the problem most closely relevant to educational concerns. Kirk viewed this problem in terms of redeeming intellectual life from the "sterility and uniformity of the mass-age."[56] We can grasp his meaning by examining the charges which he leveled against current educational and cultural practices that neglected manners and morals in favor of an unmitigated sensuality and emphasized mediocrity at the expense of the naturally talented in academic and cultural areas. The emphasis upon mediocrity was opposed on the grounds that only the few were capable of fully benefiting by a liberal arts education and that the future of society depended primarily on the development of leadership. In regard to education, the current pressure to lower academic standards was seen as an instance of the confusion of quantity with quality.

As the remedy, Kirk proposed that ethical sensibility be cultivated by the study and imitation of the lives of great individuals and by examples of elevated human character depicted in the writings of such authors as Plutarch, Dante, Montaigne, Shakespeare, Burke, and Ruskin, so that the student could acquire a sense of moral and intellectual

77

excellence. The values attained would thus bring the student an insight into the hierarchical order of the universe.[57] In addition, Kirk stressed liberal education, with high standards of selective excellence applied to all who would undertake such a program. The essential basis for the existence of academic education was deemed to lie in the attainment and dissemination of truth. Anything which interfered with this goal was to be condemned.[58]

The aim of the dissemination of truth, as Kirk conceived of it, can best be illustrated by Kirk's own words.

"By the spirit of a gentleman, Burke and Newman did not mean simply the deportment of superior rank. They meant, rather, that elevation of mind and temper, that generosity and courage of mind, which are the property of every person whose intelligence and character have been humanely disciplined. They meant that liberal education and that habit of acting upon principles which rise superior to immediate advantage and private interest, which distinguish the free man from the servile man. . . . Lacking this, Burke says, all the schooling in the world is of no avail.[59]"

To Kirk, a humane education therefore had primarily a moral significance. In fact, he conceived of *humanitas* as a whole in terms of ethical discipline. The virtues which he identified are primarily aristocratic virtues—those that have been traditionally associated with the nobility.

In considering educational questions, Kirk has devoted considerable attention to the meaning of academic freedom. He adopted W. T. Couch's definition of academic freedom as the protection of teachers from any hazards that would prevent teachers from fulfilling their obligation to pursue the truth.[60] The pursuit of truth involved the freedom of both teachers and students to express their views but excluded attempts to indoctrinate students. Kirk did not define indoctrination, but presumably he meant the systematic attempt to convert students to a particular ideology regardless of the truth of particular statements made in pursuing that objective. It would have been of considerable aid in understanding how he differentiated between freedom of expression and indoctrination had he explained his meaning of "indoctrination."

To Kirk, academic freedom pertained both to the finding and to the limited dissemination of the truth. Kirk's adherence to freedom was sharply mitigated by his lack of confidence in the old liberal view that truth would eventually prevail in competition with falsehood on the open market. He believed that this view had been based on the "foolish" conviction of the goodness and the rationality of men. In fact, Kirk believed that the ordinary citizen was often unable to distinguish between what was beneficial and what was harmful.[61] Kirk's adherence to freedom was therefore limited and qualified. For example, he felt that communists should be tolerated for the time being because they did not constitute a major threat, and because more harm would be done by censorship than by permitting them to freely express their views. He added, however, that changing circumstances could alter his stand on the matter.[62] He did advocate the censorship of pornography because he believed that pornographic literature undermined the tastes and morals of the community.[63] In subscribing to these views, Kirk was being quite consistent with his general conservative position on human nature. Since he favored curbing freedom in general, it may be very likely that his view of academic freedom was similarly limited.

It is important that we consider the general significance of his selection and treatment of the problems confronting conservatives. First, his choices of problems are interesting. The questions he asked were all of a long-term character— not ephemeral problems such as those which usually interest journalists. Furthermore, the problems chosen were not basically of a financial or economic character but were rather questions which pertained to the human needs for emotional security, responsible activity, and acceptance of a set of cogent values. To Kirk, man was a creature driven primarily by the needs of the spirit—not by economic needs nor by biological urges. In agreement with Sigmund Freud, Kirk depicted man as weak, but unlike Freud, Kirk has viewed human problems in a spiritual rather than a physical context. Furthermore, Kirk considered human nature to be an amalgam of good and evil, although he emphasized aspects of human nature which some people would regard as signs of evil but which he preferred to view as signs of weakness. To Freud, man was unequivocally evil in the sense that he conceived of man as guided primarily by selfish emotional needs. In Kirk's opinion, humans were governed more by their appetites than by their reason but he exhibited more confidence in their improvability than had Freud. Through guidance and the cultivation of a sense of emotional security, Kirk believed that men might obtain the strengths so conspicuously lacking in their nature.[64]

Of the ten problems specified by Kirk, every one with the exceptions of social justice, order, and tradition was directly based upon and was an expression of the need for moral and religious values to provide the needed guidance. Indirectly, even the three problems excepted were linked to this basic need. Two of these problems, social justice and order, were based upon the need for a clearly defined hierarchy in which each individual would find his proper place. Can it be denied that a just hierarchy must be based on a system of ordered values? Furthermore, the other problem excepted, tradition, pertained to what was in essence a means for the inculcation of values.

The causes named by Kirk for the problems confronting mankind can be reduced to four: the rise of equalitarianism, the decline of belief in moral and religious values, the extension of the power of the state, and industrialization. From a broader perspective, equalitarianism could be considered a manifestation of an implicit denial of the reality of objective values, at least with regard to the qualities of human beings. If such values exist, humans must differ in their approximation to those values; for the existence of values implies the existence of disvalues. Otherwise, we could not be aware that these values exist. If all men are equal, this implies that valuational judgments pertaining to them cannot be valid, beyond our own purely subjective preferences. This viewpoint, if valid, would also weaken the case for the existence of objective values in general. The power of the state might well be viewed as a consequence of the decline of the integrity of statesmen; the deleterious effects of industrialization might well be considered one of the contributing causes of the decline of values, with the stress on sensations, characteristic of industrialized countries, blurring the efficacy of values.

Kirk's suggested remedies can likewise be reduced to a few essential ones—the revival of faith in religious and moral values, the elevation of the standards of human achievement, and a greater reliance upon individual initiative in contrast to the present emphasis upon the state. The emphasis upon the individual would be expressed not only in greater personal responsibility but also in the encouragement of local groups and private institutions. On the whole, he was not very specific as to how to implement these remedies. Perhaps this vagueness was intentional, but at the very least a systematic discussion of the precise values which he had in mind would have been helpful. Nevertheless, Kirk's viewpoint is clear in its general purport; an emphasis upon the principle of objectively ordered moral and intellectual values, apprehended primarily through traditional usage.

Kirk's views on social problems were certainly consistent

with his general metaphysical position. Though Kirk's metaphysical views were given only in fragments, it is clear that he believed in the existence of an orderly universe based upon divine foundations. He thereby implicitly assumed the existence of a dichotomy between nature and convention, with the former conceived of as universal order and the latter conceived of in terms of violation of that natural order.[65]

To Kirk, the major purpose of education was, as we have seen, ethical in character. This purpose was to be achieved through the inculcation of understanding of the moral and intellectual order of the universe as set forth primarily in the great literary classics of the past. Such an education would presumably be based upon the coherence theory of truth since Kirk believed in the existence of an ordered interrelated universe. The student would presumably be expected to show the logical coherence and consistency of facts in relationship to one another; for order implies coherence and consistency. With regard to the organization of the curriculum, it would seem to follow that this would be based upon a prescriptive rather than an elective ordering of choices; for Kirk believed in the existence of objective values, over and beyond the personal preferences of the students involved. By application of these values, the curriculum would be determined.[66]

Before stipulating the specific subjects to be comprised in the curriculum, we should give some attention to the illative sense, a concept which Kirk borrowed from the writings of John Henry Cardinal Newman. The illative sense was described as the product of the interaction of intuition, instinct, imagination, and experience as sifted by critical reasoning. This sense, when properly exercised, contributes insights into first principles and into the ultimate foundations of authority. Kirk valued the illative sense even more highly than reason; for through its use, one could attain insight, a means of apprehension which he believed to exceed in depth the products of reason alone. This view obviously implied a stress upon those subjects through which insight could be obtained such as the arts, literature, and the drama. History could likewise provide the student with insightful experiences, especially when events are viewed in relationship to the general principles determining human conduct and their consequences. With regard to methods, imitation was important; for many insights cannot be adequately communicated by formal instruction.[67]

Kirk recommended that on the primary and secondary levels of schooling, students should concentrate on learning the techniques by which knowledge is acquired and by which the mind is employed to reason logically. Although content subjects would not be neglected, the emphasis would be on the acquisition of skills. When students reach the university level, then they could concentrate upon the study of the liberal arts; for the education of the whole man was deemed to be of greater ultimate importance than the training of the specialist. Overall, Kirk was intensely interested in the imposition of more selective standards of academic performance on all levels of instruction; for he contended that educators have emphasized mediocrity and inferiority at the expense of superiority.[68]

Typical criticisms of Kirk's ideas can be found in the comments of Gordon K. Lewis of Brandeis University and C. Wright Mills of Columbia University. Both writers questioned the practicality of Kirk's suggestions. Lewis maintained that the difficulties involved in seeking to bring a viable conservatism into existence in a non-traditional society like the United States would be virtually insurmountable. Besides, he felt that arguments based upon tradition were mere disguises for privilege.[69] To Mills, conservatism was irrelevant to American concerns; for the U.S. has no aristocracy. He doubted that one could be created.[70] He

83

maintained that the American elite lacked the cultivation and the moral elevation of a true aristocracy. According to Mills, the dominant value of the American elite was predatory success.[71]

Both Lewis and Mills repudiated conservatism on practical grounds, although Lewis also had strong doubts concerning conservative principles. As we have noted, to Lewis, conservatism was an apology for privilege whereas Mills saw several points of tension between the conservatives and the actual elite of the United States. It is evident that for Kirk to procure a sympathetic response from the American intelligentsia, he would at the very least have to specify in detail just how conservative ideals would be put into operation in a largely non-traditional society. With the exceptions of a few vague indications, he has not done this. He might well protest that he was concerned more with theory than with practice and that therefore these objections are irrelevant. This argument does not, however, change the fact that he is much more likely to see his ideals effectuated if he would design to enter the arena of prudence and practice.

Eliot and Kirk: A Comparison

Both Eliot and Kirk have reacted to the same fundamental historical trends; the decline in religious faith and in moral standards combined with the existence of strong pressures to lower academic and cultural standards. In seeking to counter these trends, both Eliot and Kirk implicitly accepted a conception of personality development based upon the importance of the interaction of the individual with society. Neither writer accepted the classical liberal faith in the autonomy of the individual. The individual must look to society as the source of his standards of behavior as well as the chief source of whatever emotional satisfactions that the individual would ever attain.

84

In seeking to counter what they viewed as the deleterious trends characteristic of their times, Eliot and Kirk utilized somewhat different approaches. Eliot stressed the basic anthropological concept, culture, while Kirk emphasized the basic sociological concept, society. Eliot wanted to know what conditions would be conducive to cultural continuity and creativity. He also wanted to uncover the aims and some of the characteristics of a Christian culture which he conceived as a society guided by Christian ideals. Kirk was intent upon dealing with the major ills which plague contemporary society. He defined most of these ills in terms of the alienation of the individual from society. Eliot and Kirk were both, however, in agreement in stressing the importance of human collectivities rather than the isolated individual.

Both Eliot and Kirk espoused traditionalism. In both cases, the traditions emphasized were primarily related to the culture and the social-institutions of the group. Eliot justified tradition primarily in terms of cultural creativity; Kirk, in terms of wisdom and the inculcation of values. Both writers believed in the importance of cultural continuity as a function of education. Both writers also believed in the importance of education as an instrument for the inculcation of moral values. They emphasized the special value of humanistic studies in the inculcation of both cultural and moral values.

Both Eliot and Kirk adhered to humanism, but they expressed their adherence in somewhat different ways. Eliot stressed the humanistic ideal of balance and applied it chiefly to cultural concerns. He also stressed literary culture, which stress was quite consistent with his aesthetic emphasis. Kirk also stressed the importance of literature, but in addition accorded an important place to intuitive insight as a function of literary studies, as evidenced by his vigorous advocacy of the existence and importance of

Newman's illative sense. As a poet, Eliot undoubtedly recognized the importance of insight but scarcely alluded to it in his writings on cultural and social issues.

Both writers were concerned about the tendency of educators to concentrate on the education of students of mediocre ability. Eliot and Kirk opposed this trend because of their belief in the limited potentialities of these students. Neither writer favored an easing of academic standards to bring higher education within the range of more students. They were both more interested in promoting and recognizing achievements rather than in the gratification of desires. Anything that would tend to undermine intellectual and cultural achievements would be likely to arouse their disapproval.

The conservative school counselor, imbued with the ideals of Eliot and Kirk, would encourage students to acquire a set of moral and religious values so that they might be better able to solve their own personal problems and at the same time so that they could achieve emotional security. He would also be concerned with providing adequate opportunities for the social integration of his charges into the wider school community. Finally, he would seek to guide students along varied educational and vocational paths in accordance with their interests and abilities.

Perhaps the most valuable educational services performed by Eliot and Kirk were to stress important aspects of education that are today generally ignored by American educators. In particular, Eliot's stress upon the importance of formal education in encouraging cultural creativity and productivity and Kirk's stress on the formal teaching of moral and spiritual values in the classroom deserve much more attention than the educational world has given. Although neither writer was very specific on implementing their educational aims, to make these suggestions in the first place is an important service. As regards the means of implementing them, Eliot has however given us important hints especially pertaining to the importance of cultural pluralism and of standards of selective excellence.

NOTES

[1]Paul O, Kristeller, *Renaissance Thought* Vol. 2 (New York: Harper and Row, 1965), p. 30.

[2]*Ibid.*, p. 41.

[3]Clarence J. Karier, *Man, Society, and Education* (Glenview Ill.: Scott, Foresman, 1967), p. 207.

[4]*Ibid.*

[5]T. S. Eliot, *Notes Towards the Definition of Culture* (New York: Harcourt Brace, 1949), preface.

[6]T. S. Eliot, *The Idea of a Christian Society* (New York: Harcourt Brace, 1940), pp. 3-4.

[7]Eliot, *Notes*, p. 104.

[8]*Ibid.*, pp. 94-95.

[9]*Ibid.*, pp. 87-88.

[10]*Ibid.*, p. 115.

[11]*Ibid.*, p. 121.

[12]*Ibid.*, p. 123.

[13]*Ibid.*, pp. 128-129.

[14]*Ibid.*, pp. 144-146.

[15]*Ibid.*, p. 157.

[16]See page 28 of this study.

[17]Eliot, *The Idea of a Christian Society*, p. 10.

[18]*Ibid.*, p. 15.

[19]*Ibid.*, p. 12.

[20]*Ibid.*, p. 12.

[21]*Ibid.*, p. 6.

[22]*Ibid.*, p. 27.

23 *Ibid.*, p. 34.

24 *Ibid.*, p. 23.

25 *Ibid.*, p. 22.

26 *Ibid.*, pp. 32-33.

27 Joad was a British philosopher and a contemporary of Eliot. He is known today for his conversion from skepticism to religious theism which occurred during his old age. See the discussion of Joad's educational ideas in Eliot's *To Criticize the Critic and Other Essays* (New York: Farrar, Straus, and Giroux, 1965), pp. 69-70.

28 Eliot, *Notes*, pp. 175, 177.

29 R. M. Hutchins, "T. S. Eliot on Education," *Measure* I (Winter, 1950), p. 3.

30 Eliot, *To Criticize the Critic*, p. 119.

31 T. S. Eliot, *Selected Essays* (New York: Harcourt, Brace, and World, 1960), p. 459.

32 Eliot, *To Criticize the Critic*, p. 85.

33 Eliot, *Notes*, p. 175.

34 Eliot, *To Criticize the Critic*, p. 89.

35 Eliot, *Notes*, p. 185.

36 *Ibid.*, p. 176.

37 Hutchins, "T. S. Eliot on Education," p. 2.

38 Eliot, *Notes*, pp. 177-179.

39 *Ibid.*, pp. 177-178. See also, Eliot, *To Criticize the Critic*, p. 103.

40 The propriety of classifying Santayana as a conservative is dubious. Santayana did not adhere to the hierarchical metaphysics characteristic of conservatives but was instead a materialistic reductionist.

41 See Russell Kirk, *The Conservative Mind* (Chicago: Henry Regnery Company, 1953), p. 6.

42 Russell Kirk, *A Program for Conservatives* (Chicago: Henry Regnery Company, 1962), pp. 16, 80.

43 *Ibid.*, pp. 41-42.

44 *Ibid.*, pp. 105-107.

45 *Ibid.*, pp. 120-121.

46 *Ibid.*, pp. 155, 161-162.

47 *Ibid.*, p. 175.

48 *Ibid.*, pp. 175-176, 180.

[49] *Ibid.*, pp. 17, 194, 201-202, 219.

[50] The speculation on how community contributes to order is my own based upon inferences from Kirk's line of thinking.

[51] Kirk, *A Program for Conservatives*, pp. 229-233.

[52] *Ibid.*, p. 229.

[53] *Ibid.*, pp. 17, 251, 255-256.

[54] On his views concerning loyalty, see *ibid.*, pp. 17, 282, 290.

[55] On tradition, see Kirk, *ibid.*,) p. 291,-299; 303-305.

[56] *Ibid.*, p. 16.

[57] *Ibid.*, pp. 59-61.

[58] Russell Kirk, *Academic Freedom* (Chicago: Henry Regnery Company, 1955), pp. 11-12.

[59] Kirk, *A Program for Conservatives*, pp. 58-59.

[60] Kirk, *Academic Freedom*, p. 1.

[61] Russell Kirk, *Beyond the Dreams of Avarice* (Chicago: Henry Regnery Company, 1956), pp. 105, 109, 114.

[62] *Ibid.*, pp. 123-124.

[63] *Ibid.*, pp. 127-128.

[64] Kirk, *A Program for Conservatives*, p. 191.

[65] *Ibid.*, pp. 41-42, 59; Kirk, *Academic Freedom*, p. 4.

[66] The content of this paragraph was based upon direct inferences from Kirk's writing rather than explicit formulations by Kirk himself.

[67] Kirk, *The Conservative Mind*, pp. 249-250.

[68] Kirk, *Academic Freedom*, p. 181.

[69] Gordon K. Lewis, "The Metaphysics of Conservatism," *The Western Political Quarterly* 6 (December, 1953), pp. 737, 744.

[70] C. Wright Mills, *The Power Elite* (New York: Oxford University Press, 1956), p. 329.

[71] *Ibid.*

CHAPTER IV

POSITIVIST HUMANISM: THE VIEWS OF IRVING BABBITT AND G. H. BANTOCK

Among influential exponents of neo-conservatism, several have espoused humanistic doctrines without a corresponding emphasis upon traditionalism. In general, these writers have been favourable to tradition and have encouraged it whenever and wherever they believed that people could still be significantly influenced by it. They have, however, preferred to rely on other means of improving society; apparently on the assumption that Western civilization has proceeded too far in the direction of the repudiation of tradition to make any large-scale reversal of the trend possible.

The positivist humanists have been concerned with the problem of finding a satisfactory means of transmission of the values generally associated with tradition which would possess the cogency that was once associated with the various cultural traditions of the world. This writer has borrowed the term, positive, from the writings of Irving Babbitt who utilized it to designate the reliance upon critical reasoning which has generally characterized the representatives of this school of thought.[1] The most influential neo-conservative writers on education who have utilized the positive humanist approach have been Irving Babbitt and G. H. Bantock. In fact there can be little doubt that Babbitt has been one of the most influential neo-conservative writers on social and cultural issues in general.

The Views of Irving Babbitt

Irving Babbitt has occupied an enigmatic place in American thought. On the one hand, he has urged what has amounted to a return to the traditional American puritan ethic; on the other hand, he has vigorously opposed those American traits which have commonly been considered to be outcomes of the acceptance of the puritan outlook, i.e., the emphasis upon commercial success and business values. In his attitudes toward religion, Babbitt also exhibited conflicting tendencies. He was sympathetic with religious goals but skeptical of the knowability of absolutes. To examine these various positions, we will consider both Babbitt's life and viewpoint. In a sense, Babbitt was both a traditionalist and a revolutionary—albeit an aristocratic rightwing revolutionary. What he rebelled against were certain characteristics of American culture. Babbitt was anything but a conformist, although the biographical material can give us only a few hints as to the origins of that non-conformity.

Babbitt was born in the summer of 1865 in the middle-western city of Dayton, Ohio, the son of Dr. Edwin Dwight Babbitt and Augusta Darling Babbitt. At the time of his son's birth, Dr. Babbitt was a partner in a business school. The elder Babbitt associated with friends of decidedly radical views. Irving later came to detest these friends of his father. One cannot help wondering whether Babbitt's subsequent hostility toward vocational education and commercialism might not have had its roots within his family. Mrs.

Babbitt died when Irving was eleven years of age. His father subsequently remarried and moved to Cincinnati where Irving and a younger sister were raised.[2]

At the age of twenty, Irving entered Harvard University where, with the exception of one year at the University of Paris, he spent his entire university student career. At the University of Paris, he studied Sanskrit and Pali with the distinguished Indic scholar, Sylvain Levi. Pali was the language in which the early Buddhist sacred writings were written. Babbitt was strongly influenced by Buddhist thought, especially by the doctrine of the Middle Path between asceticism and indulgence and by the doctrine of non-attachment to material goods.

After teaching in several colleges, Babbitt settled down to a permanent position at Harvard University. He eventually became a professor of French and comparative literature; holding this position until his death in 1933. His most famous works include *Literature and the American College* (1908) which examines problems of American education; *Rousseau and Romanticism* (1919) which is a work of literary criticism, and *Democracy and Leadership* (1924) which pertains to political theory. The same basic themes can be found in all these works. A group of distinguished associates and disciples, the neo-humanists, have diligently propagated Babbitt's views. These included Paul Elmer More, Norman Foerster, Stuart P. Sherman, W. C. Brownell and others.[3]

We can obtain an intimation of the intellectual influences which affected Babbitt by recalling that the four personages whom Babbitt named as espousing the wisdom of the ages were Aristotle, Confucius, Buddha, and Christ.[4] Of all these sages, it is probable that Aristotle exercised the strongest influence upon Babbitt due to the close resemblance of Aristotelian ideas to his own. He adopted such Aristotelian views as the conception of morality as the control of the passions and appetites by reason as well as the golden mean and the stress on contemplation. These Aristotelian views were central to Babbitt's entire philosophical approach.

Historically, Babbitt's philosophy represented a reaction against certain widespread American characteristics which were important during the early twentieth century and in some respects are even more significant today. He believed that the American people suffered from a lack of standards in some instances and, in other instances, from the confusion and inversion of standards. Babbitt attributed this situation to the American repudiation of tradition. Babbitt viewed tradition as valuable since it was a means of transmitting certain vital intellectual and moral values.[5]

The American aversion to traditionalism led to certain moral consequences which Babbitt thought to be highly undesirable. These consequences included the general spread of luxury, self-indulgence, and the increasing selfishness and avarice of special interest groups. He especially denounced the American adulation of the business community. This adulation was much more widespread before than after the Great Depression but is obviously still evident. To Babbitt, commercial avarice and cupidity undermined both intellectual and moral values.[6] The negative attitude of Babbitt and many other conservative thinkers might well surprise most Americans, many of whom have regarded conservatives as being especially favorable to commercial values but, as we have seen earlier, this widespread view was the result of confusing classical liberalism with conservatism.

Babbitt believed that the prevailing emphasis on commercial success had deleteriously affected American colleges. The tendency toward an aristocracy of money must, he felt, be counteracted by the development of an elite of wisdom and character. Yet college administrators seemed to be more interested in developing a leadership dedicated only to service and power.[7] He was also disturbed about the lack of selectivity of students in American colleges.[8] He believed that this could only detract from developing what the democracies needed most of all—a superior quality of leadership.

The America in which Babbitt lived was already beginning to slip away from the puritanical traditions of its past in favor of an increasing permissiveness. He felt that the nation was in dire need of standards of action if its ethical and intellectual integrity was to be salvaged. Since traditions no longer had the force they once commanded, these standards must be arrived at critically and on the basis of human experience. The concern to establish such standards was the basic motivation of his writing. These writings were addressed largely to those who had broken with traditional forms but still felt the need of standards.[9] The Classical and Christian traditions were deemed to be our only viable sources of standards; but in view of the predominant skepticism of the twentieth century, Babbitt reluctantly felt that standards must be arrived at critically to be convincing today.[10]

He believed the infinite to be beyond the grasp of man. The realms of being and becoming are so inextricably mixed that humans could not isolate one from the other.[11] However, he implicitly recognized the existence of the Absolute even though he denied that we could know its nature. His metaphysics, skeptical as it was, necessitated an emphasis upon psychological rather than ontological factors, if his quest for standards was to be fulfilled.

The most important distinction that we should consider in arriving at a clear understanding of Babbitt's philosophy is that between the natural self of man, which he defined in terms of impulse, and the human self, which consists of those factors which act to control impulsiveness. These factors were described in terms of separate mental faculties which were clearly indicative of Babbitt's acceptance, in at least a muted form, of faculty psychology.[12] Babbitt believed that to arrive at a condition of effective self-control, the individual should be directed by the "higher imagination" which is the faculty whereby one seized likenesses and forms conceptions. This faculty is in contrast to the "lower imagination" which is synonomous with sense perception. By means of the higher imagination, the individual can view his experiences against a backdrop of ethical values. These impressions are then tested critically through the utilization of analytical reason. The combination of the higher imagination and reason was collectively termed "insight"—a form of cognition which Babbitt rated as superior to unaided reason just as the latter was rated superior to the automatic operations of the instinctive faculty.[13] By the employment of insight, values are discriminated through reference to those constants of human history and experience which have proven themselves by their consequences.[14] The "higher will" then imposes limits on one's desires so that the insights attained can be acted upon. In contrast to the higher will, the lower will acts in accordance with desires and impulses.[15] The violation of these insights must, Babbitt maintained, eventually bring on retribution.

A basic assumption underlying his voluntaristic emphasis was that man possesses freedom of will. Otherwise, Babbitt's strictures concerning the importance of self-control would be meaningless. An important implication of his stress on personal insight into experience as the criterion for evaluation was an emphasis upon the study of history and literature, with special attention to the normative aspects of those subjects. According to this view, history is the record of the collective experience of the human species and literature consists of the imaginative reconstruction of that experience. Finally, Babbitt's faculty psychology entails a stress upon the training and discipline of one's faculties. Before we can verify these implications, we should inquire into the nature of the values which Babbitt believed that experience discloses.

Babbitt believed that the virtues of moderation, decency, and common sense worked best.[16] Fundamentally, these virtues were all characterized by Babbitt as manifestations of what he regarded as the supreme humanistic virtue, decorum—the disciplining of impulses to the proportions discerned by the ethical imagination.[17] These proportions would be obtained in turn by reflection upon past human experiences.

In political affairs, the supreme virtue was considered to be justice which Babbitt defined in terms of rendering to each individual what was due him in accordance with the amount and the quality of his endeavor.[18] This is essentially a proportionate or relational concept of justice which is based on the assumption that men contribute unequally to the welfare of society. In addition, an implied assumption seems to be present that equality is undesirable or unattainable. To Babbitt, it seemed obvious that justice could not be attained until people learn to act in accordance with standards for determining how things should be apportioned. Humility was therefore considered to be the root of justice and all other virtues; for humility, as Babbitt employed the term, consisted of the willingness to look up to and to imitate standards. In this regard, he had great respect for religious creeds and religious institutions. To Babbitt, the chief virtue of the churches was the peace that they instilled in their congregations through teaching the submission to a higher will.[19] Thus, Babbitt, an ardent skeptic, approached the Christian conception of Grace. As to the end of moral behavior, Babbitt posited no supernaturalistic goal since this would be inconsistent with his epistemological skepticism. He posited instead the limited goal of temporal happi-

97

ness. Unfortunately, he did not define happiness. Since he held that happiness could only be obtained by the disciplining of the impulses, we can assume that he referred to the Aristotelian conception of happiness, a sense of satisfaction obtained by doing one's work well. As is well-known, Aristotle meant by doing one's work well activity of the soul in accordance with moral and intellectual virtue which in the case of man pertained to the activity of reason. Hence, happiness for human beings would consist ultimately of living in accordance with reason. To live in this way, it is essential that feelings and impulses be kept under control.

To Babbitt, primitivism, the arch-enemy of humanism, was especially exemplified by the works of Rousseau.[20] Babbitt equated primitivism with spontaneity which was considered to be the antithesis of discipline.[21] Babbitt's attitude toward spontaneity is shown in his classification of the forms of knowledge which were distinguished in terms of the psychological faculties involved. Instinct, which pertained to impulse and feeling, was rated below reason which was deemed to be primarily an analytical faculty. Both instinct and reason were rated below insight which pertained to the immediate apprehension of reality. This apprehension was attributed to the imagination which ideally worked in collaboration with reason, the latter faculty being employed to scrutinize the apprehensions obtained. Since Babbitt believed the imagination to be the faculty which governs mankind, he felt it to be vitally important that the imagination agree with reason rather than with the expansive desires. He believed that the latter situation caused most of the evil existing in the world.[22] In spite of his disclaimers, it can be argued that Babbitt was really a disguised rationalist; for, according to Babbitt, reason should be the final judge concerning the truth of our ethical perceptions. Instinct was thus associated with primitivism, while reason without imagination was linked to a pedantic rationalism. For educational theorists, one of the most important implications of Babbitt's position was his anxiety to avoid confusing the planes of being. He was especially disturbed over the primitivists' confusion of instinct with insight which had, Babbitt thought, resulted in their most grievous errors, such as the equation of beauty with lust and of awe with wonder. As we shall see later, Babbitt was vitally concerned with developing the powers of discrimination of college students so that they could avoid this confusion.

For Babbitt, the primitivistic dichotomy between the individuals' natural goodness and the repressiveness of society was erroneous. Like Aristotle, Babbitt believed that the individual reaches his perfection in society. Because of his skepticism concerning the natural goodness and wisdom of the individual, he condemned the child-centered curriculum so eagerly propounded by the educational naturalists and their allies. He maintained that instead of being guided by youthful whims, the educational process should be directed toward the super-personal goals of wisdom and character—wisdom, in the sense of standards of moral and intellectual value; character as expressed in the will to act in accordance with those standards.[23] In common with the Buddhists, Babbitt believed that human nature was not so much depraved as lazy. Give the individual the power to determine the nature of the curriculum, and then see how many elect the least demanding courses.[24] In his opinion, no satisfactory substitute existed for the imposition of the disciplinary activity of the higher will upon the recalcitrant desires of youth.

Babbitt was most concerned with collegiate instruction. It was at this level that, he believed, the essential effort should be undertaken to develop the critical, discriminatory powers of the individual student. In contrast, the basic function of the lower schools was to transmit knowledge and the graduate school was to be devoted to productive scholarship.[25] Hence, Babbitt would certainly have been hostile toward the recurring suggestion that the American college be abolished by integrating the first two years with the high school and the last two years with the graduate school. To Babbitt, the college had a unique function which transcended in importance the functions of both the secondary school and the graduate school. In such a perspective, the abolition of the college would obviously constitute a major tragedy.

To Babbitt, the college had to be selective in its admissions policies if it was to properly perform its function. The expertise of relating ideas well is rare, and wastefulness would be the consequence of attempting to educate individuals of inadequate potential. Implicit in this position is the assumption that the cultivation of leadership is of greater importance than the uplift of the masses. Where the interests of the two conflict, those of the individuals who exhibit the greatest potentiality must be held paramount. To Babbitt, the development of superior leadership was of crucial importance; for upon this process depended the future welfare of society. When considering the aims of the college, Babbitt was quite explicit:

"Even though the whole world seem (*sic*) bent on living the quantitative life, the college should remember that its business is to make of the graduates men of quality in the real and not the conventional meaning of the term. In this way it will do its share toward creating that aristocracy of character and intelligence that is needed in a community like ours to take the place of an aristocracy of birth, and to counteract the tendency toward an aristocracy of money. A great deal is said nowadays about the democratic spirit that should pervade our colleges. This is true if it means that the college should be in profound sympathy with what is best in democracy. It is false if it means, as it often does, that the college should level down and suit itself to the point of view of the average individual. . . . But from the standpoint of the college one thoroughly cultivated person should be more to the purpose than a hundred persons who are only partly cultivated."[26]

Regarding his views on the college curriculum, it is important to emphasize that Babbitt rejected the elective system that was so enthusiastically championed by Charles Eliot, President of Harvard University where Babbitt taught. To Babbitt, the notion that all subjects are of equal value was anathema. Furthermore, unlike his superior at Harvard, Babbitt had little confidence in the ability of late adolescents to make judicious choices. Instead, as we have previously noted, he felt that the native human indolence of the teen-ager would assert itself in the selection of courses to the detriment of academic standards.[27] In this respect, Babbitt consistently applied his general views on human nature to an important educational issue. Yet, on this as on so many other issues, Babbitt was exceedingly vague. He neglected to specify in detail the studies that he would require. We can, however, obtain a few indications by examining his arguments for the teaching of the Greek and Roman classics.

Perhaps the most important justification given by Babbitt for the study of the classics was that ancient Greco-Roman literature represented the most perfect fusion of reason with imagination and therefore appealed to what is the most universal and eternal in human nature.[28] What he meant by this remark can be grasped by reference to his general philosophical position. Babbitt desired the fusion of reason with imagination for the purpose of discerning the ethical universals and their influence upon human nature. As was previously observed, this viewpoint leads implicitly to a stress upon the study of history and literature with special emphasis upon the general normative principles inferred therefrom. To Babbitt, the primary criterion for the selection of courses of study was their value in bringing to students a knowledge of those constants of human experience which have proven to be of the greatest worth as guideposts of human conduct. Therefore, the teacher imbued with the ideals of Babbitt would stress the importance of general ideas and would treat historical events and great works of literature in relationship to normative principles.

It might occasion some surprise to find that another justification given by Babbitt for the study of classical literature was that it exhibited greater objectivity than modern writings; for Babbitt's prescriptions appear to sanction subjectivity.[29] Yet, when Babbitt's value theory is fully comprehended, this justification no longer seems to be inconsistent with other statements made by Babbitt for he felt that ethical standards should be arrived at by a dispassionate and critical consideration of human experience. The important consideration pertaining to academic objectivity was the means whereby the teacher reached his conclusions, not whether a partisan view was presented to his class, for Babbitt implicitly sanctioned the latter.

To Babbitt, modern literature was marred by the indulgence of its practitioners in "sentimental and romantic revery rather than in a resolute and manly grappling with the plain facts of existence."[30] In contrast, classical literature was valued for its ethical insights, supposedly arrived at by the cooperation of the higher reason with the imagination.[31] What Babbitt meant by the "higher reason" was the analytical faculty which acted upon the imagination. It is quite evident that to Babbitt the axiological aspects of education were paramount.

Of nearly equal importance among Babbitt's motivations for emphasizing classical literature was the disciplinary value derived from mastering the precise meanings of the words of the ancients. This process promotes the habit of serious intellectual effort while the drill in style obtained from translating classical writings was felt to be a superior means of mastering English.[32] This stress upon discipline and drill is congruent with Babbitt's basic psychology which was based upon the assumption of the existence of distinct faculties which had implicitly to be trained to function well. Therefore, Babbitt emphasized the value of the classics for the skills which they engendered as well as for the ethical insights which they conveyed.

Finally, by viewing contemporary events in the perspective of the distant past, the individual could become more sensitive to the dangers of the present. In particular, the fatuous optimism which still pervaded America during most of the duration of Babbitt's life might thereby be corrected.[33] By the stress upon the value of the study of the classics in viewing the present, Babbitt probably had in mind that phase of Roman history when the Roman republic was being transformed into the tyranny of the Caesars. It is common knowledge that conservative writers have been concerned about a possible reoccurrence of this trend through such tendencies as the mounting disrespect for law and the spread of socialism. Liberals and radicals have on the whole been much more sanguine about the future. The differences which exist on this issue stem from basically different assumptions concerning the flexibility of human nature.

Babbitt characterized his general position by contrasting it with the two chief antithetical viewpoints: those of the "philologists" and of the "dilettantes." The former delight in the minute accumulation of facts with little or no concern for their significance. The latter stress the thrill obtained through cultivating aesthetic sensations and sanction a kind of emotional indolence. Babbitt believed that the philologists constituted the most serious menace because they dominated the departments of history and literature in

103

American colleges. In contrast to both these groups, he mentioned the "humanists" whom he characterized as the advocates of disciplining students in the intelligent utilization of ideas—especially, of the relationships between literary concepts and normative values.[34] As an example, he esteemed the French doctorate as the embodiment of humanistic ideals in contrast to the American doctorate which, according to Babbitt, fundamentally embodied philological values.[35] Only by the adoption of standards on a par with the French doctorate or the Oxford first-class honors degree could American higher education have a constructive impact upon contemporary problems.

Babbitt was fundamentally a very repetitious writer, dealing with the same themes in book after book with minor differences in expansiveness and in sequence. His writing is studded with brilliant insights but is highly unsystematic in character. In particular, he had the annoying habit of making assertions without expanding upon them, either by careful formulation of definitions or by sustained step by step argumentation. These practices have resulted in a widespread misunderstanding of his basic thesis. This misunderstanding has been most unfortunate; for he had focused on one of the most important problems confronting American education today—the need to develop and inculcate standards of moral and intellectual evaluation. He has also realized that if standards are to be living realities, there must be discipline and selectivity in accordance with these standards. Whether his prescriptions are adequate is another question; but his ability to focus on the central problem and to free himself from the effects of the indoctrination which Americans generally undergo from their early youth make him, in the opinion of this writer, a highly significant figure even though his writings may not be models of systematic scholarship.

In his general educational position, Irving Babbitt was

more than anything else a humanist. For him the fundamental goal of education was to develop among students the ability to discriminate among moral and intellectual values in terms of their varying degrees of excellence and to thereby achieve a sense of harmony and proportion. His concern was even more with the ethical than with the intellectual although his standards for judging the ethical were both aesthetic and rational. His stress upon harmony and proportion was fundamentally aesthetic while the role that he assigned to reason as the final arbitrator of the insights established by the ethical imagination mark Babbitt as a rationalist, even though he considered himself to be primarily a voluntarist.

Babbitt's view of man as primarily guided by the imagination is very significant; for it indicates that he believed that human knowledge originates, either primarily or exclusively, from sense perception. As earlier noted, he defined imagination as sense perception (the lower imagination) or as the faculty which stores and relates sense perceptions (the higher imagination). This is an educationally significant position; for it implies that the classroom teacher should begin instruction with concrete materials, even when he is dealing with abstract concepts. Babbitt's emphasis upon literature in the teaching of normative concepts is easily explainable from this viewpoint as providing the needed concrete exemplifications to form a basis for value judgments. In contrast, the teacher who believes that normative judgments are based primarily upon innate ideas, would be more likely to convey the nature of normative judgments in the form of abstract principles. One would thus be more likely to teach normative judgments directly rather than through literature.

In his emphasis upon literature and the imagination as well as in his stress upon harmony and proportion, Babbitt was most definitely a humanist. He was also humanistic in his emphasis upon the development of the individual rather than the group. The major problem here is how to reconcile this position with the fact that like most other conservatives Babbitt considered the individual to be fundamentally a social creature and not an autonomous entity. Although, as far as this writer is aware, Babbitt has not dealt with this problem, it can be resolved easily on the basis of Babbitt's general philosophical position and that of Aristotle, the fundamental source upon whom Babbitt apparently relied in the formulation of his viewpoint. Man is a social animal in that he requires society in order to reach his perfection. However, the fundamental problems which interfere with the happiness of the individual are primarily individual rather than social in character. The individual must first accept a standard of values and then abide by them before he can contribute meaningfully to the solution of social problems. In essence, Babbitt's criterion of individual excellence pertained to the individual's willingness to view things in ethical perspective and to act on the basis of the insights obtained. To do this intelligently, the individual needed to acquire the competency of discriminating between values with facility and dexterity. After he accomplished this task, he could then worry about his own adjustment to society and about the improvement of society.

Although Babbitt viewed tradition favorably, he felt, as we have seen, that Americans had moved too far from their traditional roots to resort to tradition on any but the most limited basis. Instead, he preferred to rely upon the development of an elite characterized by the understanding and application of standards of critical judgment. He believed that such an elite could provide the reliable value standards that had once been provided through tradition.

The general reaction to the ideas of Babbitt and his colleagues mirrored the prevalent climate of opinion among the intellectuals of the period between the two world wars. Although Babbitt had been writing for several decades previously, his work was not subjected to widespread written criticism until about 1930. Some critics, such as Allan Tate and T. S. Eliot, were generally sympathetic to his views but they felt that the values which Babbitt espoused required a religious orientation to be convincing. They were thus questioning the cogency of combining Babbitt's ethical humanism with his well-known religious skepticism.[36] Other critics, such as Edmund Wilson and Malcolm Cowley, reacted against Babbitt's constant emphasis upon the will to refrain from and to control the passions. Both Wilson and Cowley found this viewpoint to be lacking in warmth and compassion. Cowley, in particular, typified those writers who rejected what they felt to be the aristocratic snobbery and priggish moralism of Babbitt and his allies.[37]

The most frequent reaction of Babbitt's critics was to reject his philosophy on the ground of Babbitt's hostility toward scientific naturalism. As is well-known, Babbitt had insisted on a sharp separation between humans and the lower animals on the ground that humans possessed the ability to control their impulses. Because of this position, Babbitt maintained that the methods of the physical and the biological sciences were not fully applicable to human beings. Such famous writers as Lewis Mumford, Henry Hazlitt, and C. Hartley Grattan were outspokenly hostile toward Babbitt's separation of humanity from the other aspects of nature. Lewis Mumford felt that Babbitt's emphasis upon "the will to refrain" was really an attempt to protect people from vigilence and responsibility by dodging the risks involved in expressing one's emotions.[38] Hazlitt denied that the ability to control one's impulses was something peculiarly human. He also denied that humans could separate themselves absolutely from other creatures in their ordinary habits of life. Hazlitt maintained that a man cannot be even a humanist unless he has recently done something so bestial as eating a meal.[39] Grattan denied the cogency of Babbitt's separation of humans from other forms of animal life on the ground that the mind, presumably the basis of human acts, was a biological organ.[40] Grattan had evidently confused the mind with the brain. The brain is certainly a biological organ but the mind, insofar as it differs from the brain, is obviously not a biological organ. To make his argument convincing, Grattan would have to prove that the mind and the brain are synonymous. Beyond making an assertion of their equivalency, Grattan has not even attempted to prove this point. In any case, it is evident that naturalism dominated the thinking of most of Babbitt's critics. It is also evident that few of them presented reasoned arguments against Babbitt's views. Reactions, such as those of Wilson and Cowley, seem to this writer, to be at least as emotional as intellectual. To say that Babbitt was cold or snobbish really amounts to mere name-calling unless the namers specify precisely what they mean, give evidence to substantiate their charges, and show why such traits are undesirable.

Roman Catholic writers and scholars were one group that came to Babbitt's defense. The ideas of Babbitt that had antagonized so many intellectuals elicited a sympathetic response among many Roman Catholics who were attracted by Babbitt's condemnation of naturalism and his belief in absolute moral standards.[41] There were some strong affinities that existed between some of Babbitt's views and those of the Thomists. Babbitt shared the same Aristotelian heritage as did St. Thomas. However, Babbitt was apparently more influenced by Buddhism and by religious skepticism than by Christianity. In spite of the wide divergence between Babbitt and the Thomists on religious beliefs, striking similarities can be found in the dimension of values such as the common emphasis of both on temperance and humility. However, Thomists ultimately grounded values on supernatural foundations while Babbitt utilized a basically positivistic approach.

The marked tendency of educational writers to distinguish between Babbitt and contemporary neo-conservatives has no basis in fact. Babbitt was reacting against the same fundamental tendencies which have alarmed contemporary conservative intellectuals: the undermining of traditional standards and the spread of equalitarianism. The educational and social reforms advocated by Babbitt would also generally have the assent of present-day conservatives. The period in which Babbitt wrote was not really very different from the present period of history. The basic problems, such as the spread of moral and religious skepticism and of equalitarianism, are today much the same as they were fifty years ago but with the important difference that today they are much more pressing. The problems that Irving Babbitt concerned himself with are still very much with us.

The Views of G. H. Bantock

Like Babbitt, the British educational philosopher G. H. Bantock exemplifies the same basic combination of the humanist with so-called "positive" ideas. As will be indicated later, there were some basic differences between the views expressed by Bantock and Babbitt.

A faculty member of the University of Leicester in England, G. H. Bantock was originally trained in philosophy and literature. He has attributed his close attention to the intricacies of language to his training in those disciplines.[42] A prolific writer on educational problems, his best known works include *Freedom and Authority in Education* (1955), *Education in an Industrial Society* (1963), *Education and*

109

Values (1965), and *Education, Culture, and the Emotions* (1967).

The particular historical trends which most influenced G. H. Bantock were similar to those which have had an impact on other neo-conservative writers. He believed that the most serious educational and social problem was the need for an authority that would give meaning to life. He maintained that since World War I there has been a concerted effort to substitute individual desires for objective moral values. The latter were transmitted by tradition while the movement to undermine these values was basically a reaction against the war.[43] While we might quarrel with Bantock's chronology and rationale for the existence of this trend, there is little doubt that such a tendency exists and that it became especially widespread after World War I.

Bantock was also alarmed by the spread of both meritocracy and equalitarianism. As we pointed out previously, the trend toward meritocracy, or the policy of providing responsible positions and advanced schooling solely on indications of competency, has been more widespread in Britain than in the United States where educational equalitarianism has had a greater impact. Bantock contended that meritocracy led to the apotheosis of the narrow specialist and to the consequent decline of general education and high cultivation.[44] It also has resulted in the lowering of the general tone of society and the decline of *noblesse oblige*.[45]

Alongside the trend to meritocracy and often confused with it has been the trend toward educational equalitarianism. Universal literacy was considered to be one of the basic causes for the rise of this equalitarianism since it encouraged the development of an enormous mass culture, dominated by the intellectually unqualified whose combined pressure has tended to lower the level of intellectual skills.[46] Other causes named by Bantock included the spread of progressive education, comprehensive secondary

110

schools, and related tendencies. Bantock implicitly took the position that the education of the academically talented was more important than the education of the academically mediocre. He also implied that the intellectual uplift of the masses to the point where they would be able to appreciate and contribute to high culture was either an impossibility or could be accomplished only through the sacrifice of optimum development of the most talented.

In his response to these trends, Bantock was influenced by the writings of Cardinal Newman, Matthew Arnold, D. H. Lawrence, and most especially T. S. Eliot.[47] He has written studies of Cardinal Newman and of Arnold. He especially praised Cardinal Newman for his emphasis on the importance of objective values and Matthew Arnold for his attack on the degeneration of standards caused by the impact of mechanistic and materialistic philosophies.[48] The means whereby Bantock was influenced by the two twentieth century aesthetes, Lawrence and Eliot, can be gleaned from the comments of Bantock himself. For example, Bantock praised Lawrence's emphasis on affective education and emphasized the same aspect himself. Bantock also praised and was influenced by Eliot's emphasis upon education as a cultural rather than a political phenomenon.[49] In his general methodology, Bantock was also influenced by two British literary critics, I. A. Richards and F. R. Leavis, from whom he learned to be suspicious of abstractions divorced from the concrete realities of "the human situation."[50] In general, the sources cited by Bantock consisted chiefly of British conservatives with a great concern for educational and cultural quality. Most of these writers were critical of both the philosophical and common forms of materialism.

In identifying the aims of education, Bantock used a basically cultural approach. He began by defining the nature of culture, which he conceived of as the social, emotional, and intellectual "structures" inherited from the past. These structures, transmitted in the forms of conventions, patterns, and models, function to enhance the opportunities for expression and to make explicit what is permissible so as to inhibit "exhausting hankerings and time-absorbing aspirations."[51] Bantock's terminology is significant; for it indicates his desire to order both academic learning and affective experiences so that students could learn to perceive the underlying patterns. The emphasis upon patterns indicates that Bantock probably accepted a coherence theory of truth; for the essence of this theory is consistency which implies an integration of parts with one another (pattern).

In the most general terms, Bantock defined the school as an agency whose primary function was cognitive in character. The test of the excellence of the school was considered to be the degree to which it increased the knowledge and understanding of the students. Since he viewed feeling as an avenue of cognition, his attention to emotional education was not in conflict with his primary concern.[52] To Bantock, the school was essentially a cultural institution whose primary function was to release thought and thus facilitate individual expression. In the performance of these functions the school has to impose constraints upon individual freedom. These constraints were however justified as necessary if the school was to perform efficiently the specific tasks of imparting understandings, developing important skills, and cultivating "some refined modes of feeling."[53]

To demarcate the functions of the school more clearly, it is essential to discuss Bantock's opposition to those who have sought to over-extend the area of academic endeavor. He especially resented the efforts of educators who sought to include mental hygiene among the functions of the teacher since he believed that teachers are generally incom-

112

petent to practice psychological therapy. Furthermore, mental therapists are primarily concerned with the pathological while teachers should be more concerned with the problems of children in the real world. Even more disturbing to Bantock was the tendency toward permissiveness which has resulted from confusing the roles of the teacher and the therapist. Like Eliot and other conservative writers, Bantock believed that tension is a positive and desirable state in maximizing achievement. Therapists are concerned with the problem of reducing tension, but, when teachers attempt to do the same thing by reducing academic requirements, the consequence is to lower the quality of scholastic endeavor. He admitted, however, that equalitarian and anti-authoritarian factors have also undermined standards.[54]

Some American college professors have invoked the mental health of the student as a justification for avoiding the awarding of low grades to students who would otherwise have received them. The usual explanation given is that students would suffer unnecessarily from the receipt of low grades.[55] On Bantock's principles, this argument would be fallacious since not only are most educators unqualified to render such judgments, but they also undermine an important incentive to achievement and actually contribute to the current erosion of academic standards. The differences between Bantock and those who have disagreed with his position on this matter can to a large extent be attributed to differing views as to what motivates students to achieve academically. Furthermore, to Bantock and other conservatives, achievement is more important than contentment. In fact, achievement often brings contentment.

Bantock did not, however, repudiate the utilization of emotions in the classroom. Quite the contrary! He argued for a greater emphasis upon the emotions in education but

113

definitely not in the manner of the Rousseauistic naturalists. What Bantock wanted was not spontaneous self-expression but rather "a mode of structuring, a means to order, an elaboration and a making" with the emphasis placed upon the product rather than the self.[56]

To comprehend just exactly what Bantock meant, it is important to understand his conception of the nature of the emotions; for he viewed them not just as passive states but rather as active acts of conscience. To Bantock, emotions were outward expressions of one's assessments of situations. There therefore existed both correct and incorrect responses to a situation. Bantock merged the emotional with the cognitive and by so doing implied that emotional problems could, at least to some degree, be dealt with academically.[57]

The teacher's role in the education of the emotions was to instruct students to discriminate between the various kinds of emotion.[58] The teacher would do this partly by example through refraining from indulging in coarse or vulgar emotions. Furthermore, students would learn to discriminate between different kinds of feeling by the study of literature and the fine arts. In fact, Bantock felt that literature and the arts are more important than the sciences since they are concerned with values and passions—matters which are more basic than those which pertain to the sciences. He recommended that some acquaintanceship with literature and the arts be required of all educated men but that the only scientific knowledge that educated laymen really needed pertained to the scientific method.[59]

Bantock's attitudes toward the emotions are very significant in exemplifying the essential contrast between educational conservatives and Rousseauistic naturalists on the scope of formal schooling. To assert as many writers have, that conservatives favor an exclusively academic type of schooling while their opponents place greater stress upon

114

non-intellectual factors is to overstate the difference that actually exists on this matter. Every conservative thinker that we have dealt with in this study has been concerned not only with formal academic education but also with the broader implications and functions of the educational process. Conservatives do obviously stress academic education to a greater extent than do either the adherents of the naturalistic wing or the experimentalist wing of the progressive movement. However, affective education also concerns them. The true contrast is between an emphasis upon a highly structured academic situation and one in which spontaneity is emphasized. As a group, conservatives have no wish either to extirpate or to ignore emotions. Their concern is with disciplining and ordering emotions to the values discerned by the intellect. They are quite willing to deal with emotional problems but only to the degree that these problems can be handled cognitively. They have no wish to broaden the scope of formal education to include therapeutic functions of the kind which are normally performed by psychiatrists, psychologists, and psychiatric social workers. Some progressives believe that greater spontaneity would be highly desirable in education. Conservatives emphatically disagree with this view. They look upon the stress on spontaneity as tending toward permissiveness. As a group, they feel that there is far too much permissiveness in education already for the good of either the student or the larger community of which he is a member.

In common with many other conservatives, Bantock has expressed strong disapproval of the child-centered concept of learning. He believed that this concept rests upon the assumption of the natural goodness of man when left to develop uncontaminated by society. He criticized this view on two grounds: that isolation of the individual from social pressures is not possible and that children are not competent to make the important decisions needed to determine

115

the methods and content of academic instruction. In determining what to teach children, their powers and potential should be considered, but most children are not fully aware of what potentialities they do possess, nor do they have a clear idea of how these powers can be utilized by society. The individual child should be nurtured to broaden the range of his experience and to quiet his rebellious nature. In Bantock's view, interest should not be an important consideration. A task in which a child might not be interested might prove to be very interesting once the child begins to do it. The teacher should definitely be the expert and the guide. Nevertheless, the powers and potentialities of the individual child should be taken into account so that in substance Bantock was urging not a one-sided teacher-centered system but rather interaction between teacher and students.[60]

Bantock felt that the educational progressives have been so zealous in promoting the happiness of children that they have overlooked the value and importance of academic learning. In contrast, Bantock has expressed a preference for achievement over immediate happiness.[61] In the end, he confidently believed that achievement will prove to be more satisfying than immediate gratification.[62] Like Aristotle, Bantock believed that reason is the supreme characteristic of man and that life lived in rational terms is necessary for the best life.[63] To the charge that control over children would undermine their freedom, he opposed a positive conception of freedom as the following quotation clearly indicates:

"Just, then, as social freedom springs out of the acceptance of the moral law, so the freedom to perform various skills and to make sense of the world around us so that we can move about it, springs from the acceptance of and submission to the authority inherent in the various bodies of human learning. And it is a fact of human experience

116

that the 'subjects' within which, in the course of time, we learn to move with the greatest assurance and freedom are not necessarily those which we are at first most 'interested' by or 'enjoy.' "[64]

Freedom was therefore viewed not simply as the absence of restraints but rather as the ability to accomplish various tasks. For this, restraint is required rather than permissiveness. The foregoing quotation is also indicative of Bantock's acceptance of traditional subject-matter boundaries in preference to the more integrated approaches of educational progressives. Elsewhere, he defended subject-matter boundaries as imposed by the nature of the material studied.[65]

Although Bantock emphasized the cognitive functions of education even when dealing with affective approaches, he did not feel that a single set of aims should be applied throughout the educational system. The level of intelligence and the degree of motivation varied too much to render a single set of educational aims practical.[66] Apparently, he assumed that efforts to change intellectual and motivational levels to any significant degree would be doomed to failure. Presumably, Bantock recognized the importance of both heredity and early upbringing.[67] The educator must, therefore, study the nature of his students and adjust his teaching accordingly. The utopian hopes of some educational thinkers would evidently seem to those inspired by Bantock's ideas to be visionary and impractical.

Unlike such other conservatives as Irving Babbitt and T. S. Eliot, Bantock devoted special attention to the education of the less gifted. Other conservatives had, by not prescribing any special academic program for the less academically inclined, tacitly assumed that beyond the level of basic literacy, the needs of these children could best be met by practical experience. As a group, conservatives most definitely favored selective admissions policies on the higher, and, in

117

some instances, even the secondary level of education. Bantock certainly agreed with his fellow conservatives that access to the universities and to academic curricula in general should be restricted to the academically gifted and motivated. On the other hand, he believed that classroom teaching could be meaningful for the less gifted provided that ample provision is made for taking into account the intellectual characteristics of these children. In general, this approach seems quite different from that of the educational equalitarians who are now especially influential in American education. The latter believe that the masses have the capacity for understanding and profiting from an academic type of education and that their relatively poor performance is due either to poor teaching, deficient early cultural upbringing, or discrimination. Therefore, they have developed various different kinds of plans to equalize educational opportunity through providing special attention for the "culturally deprived." It is common knowledge among educators that children have shown some improvement as a result of special teaching, but there is considerable doubt concerning the permanence of the changes made.[68] The conservative contention in this regard is that the effort, time, and money expended would have produced greater and more lasting dividends if greater attention had been given to the academically promising. In essence, this difference in attitude is based upon a striking difference of viewpoint pertaining to the relative flexibility of human nature.

Bantock believed that efforts made to transform the less gifted into intellectuals were doomed to failure; for the non-academic child lives in a different world from his more scholarly counterpart. The crux of the difference pertains to the degree of ability and understanding manifested in the utilization of abstract concepts and the written word. From Bantock's point of view, the less academically able child was believed to be living in a predominantly oral

118

world. The interests of this child were believed to lie in matters relating to his local environment and the marvelous. When the child reads, it is for the story and not for either self-improvement or explanation.

The type of education suitable for this kind of child should differ fundamentally from that of the academically gifted child. On the secondary level, the education of the less able forty percent, excluding the "sub-normal," must be centered on the practical and the concrete if it is to be meaningful. Such academic subjects as foreign languages, formal history, and geography should be dropped from the course of study that this type of child should pursue. In addition, the amount of time devoted to mathematics should be diminished. English would be taught as well as good citizenship but the latter would be learned through cooperative activity rather than by formal instruction. What historical and geographical material that Bantock would keep would be incidental to the learning of other subjects.

The non-academic child would learn art by proceeding from the study of "pop" culture to more academic matters. The study of music might begin with calypso; of the visual arts, with the study of films. The chief purpose of teaching art and music to the non-academic children would be to enable them to employ their leisure constructively.

A large portion of the time spent by these children in school would be devoted to vocational purposes. The boys would learn such tasks as plumbing, paper-hanging, boot mending, and gardening while the girls would study dietetics, mothercraft, cooking, needlework, and kindred subjects. In other words, Bantock felt that the school should prepare these children for the vocations that they would be most likely to pursue later in life.[69]

In general, Bantock had recommended that many of the practices associated with progressive and vocational education be applied to the needs of the less gifted children.

119

Where he differed with John Dewey was in the latter's insistence that an essentially practical type of education be given to children on all levels of ability. Bantock was highly critical of Dewey's emphasis on the practical; for one's immediate needs tend to be fleeting, and Dewey had apparently forgotten that the detection of a problem is dependent on anterior assumptions which are often non-empirical in character.[70] Bantock did not therefore prefer practical education but felt compelled to advocate it for the less gifted because of the educational limitations of the latter.

With regard to children on the high-average level of academic development, Bantock recommended the pursuance of a technical education although some general education courses would also be included. The latter would pertain essentially to literature and the arts.[71] Students, on the higher levels of academic ability, would attend training colleges if they lack motivation while those who possess both motivation and ability would be prepared for entrance into the universities. The training colleges would differ from the universities in that the former would devote themselves exclusively to teaching without the research function of the university.[72]

In essence, Bantock advocated a class system of education but one which was not based on the class affiliations of the families of the students but rather on the academic capabilities and the motivations of the individuals involved. Yet, he was not really advocating a pure meritocracy; for elsewhere in his writings one finds that he deplored the rise to power of individuals of high intelligence without cultivated manners and refined morals.[73] In any case, he recommended, in substance, that the schools serve as agencies of selection for the various occupational levels of society. This position clearly implies the prime importance of academic ability as the selective factor. Those who possess the requisite amount of this ability would qualify for the most prestigious positions. Others would be prepared for less demanding positions based on their relative performance on various measures of academic ability and motivation. One might well wonder whether these other occupations do not demand special talents as well for the efficient performance of duties. An academic incompetent is not necessarily mechanically competent.

Babbitt and Bantock Compared

Both Babbitt and Bantock were reacting primarily in opposition both to the decline of traditional authority and the permeation of contemporary culture by equalitarianism. Of the two, Babbitt showed a hostility toward business values which Bantock failed to exhibit. This contrast may reflect differences between the British and American social climates; for business values have generally been more influential in the United States than in the United Kingdom.

Both of the protagonists of positive humanism felt that belief in objective values could be restored by an educational system in which the most important aim would be to teach students to discriminate between values. Bantock emphasized in particular the importance of discrimination between the passions in terms of the values which they exemplified.

As humanists, Babbitt and Bantock both appreciated the importance of literature and of imaginative insight in general. In addition, Babbitt stressed the value of harmony and proportion as social ideals. Both men recognized the value of tension. Bantock openly espoused this value while it was an implicit assumption of Babbitt's stress on voluntaristic discipline. Both writers were definitely achievement-oriented. In this as in other respects, they contrast strikingly

121

with the predominant trend of American education today. Bantock's viewpoint should be of especial interest to those educators concerned about the issues raised concerning the controversy between the exponents of mass education and those of selective education beyond the elementary level of schooling. Bantock has offered us a third alternative with regard to the academically incompetent; extended formal education on a simplified non-conceptual level.

NOTES

[1]Irving Babbitt, *Rousseau and Romanticism* (New York: Meridian Books, 1953), p. 5.

[2]See the account given by Dora Babbitt in Frederick Manchester and Odell Shepherd, eds., *Irving Babbitt: Man and Teacher* (New York: Putnam's, 1941), pp. ix and x. The entire book is a gold mine of information on Irving Babbitt.

[3]Perhaps the most influential work produced by a member of this group was Paul Elmer More's *Aristocracy and Justice* (1915).

[4]Irving Babbitt, *Democracy and Leadership* (Boston: Houghton Mifflin Company, 1924), p. 163.

[5]*Ibid.*, pp. 240-241.

[6]*Ibid.*, pp. 19, 272.

[7]Irving Babbitt, *Literature and the American College* (Chicago: Henry Regnery Company, 1956), p. 71.

[8]*Ibid.*, pp. 53, 71.

[9]Babbitt, *Democracy and Leadership*, p. 34.

[10]Irving Babbitt, *Criticism in America: Its Function and Status* (New York: Harcourt Brace, 1924), p. 164.

[11]Irving Babbitt, *On Being Creative* (Boston: Houghton Mifflin Company, 1932), pp. xxvii-xxviii.

[12]Irving Babbitt, *Rousseau and Romanticism*, pp. 26-27, 51; *Democracy and Leadership*, pp. 11, 14.

[13]For the nature of the higher imagination see Babbitt, *Democ-*

racy and Leadership, p. 10; on the nature of insight see Babbitt, *Rousseau and Romanticism*, p. 47.

[14]Babbitt, *On Being Creative*, p. xxxviii.

[15] *Ibid.*, p. xix.

[16] *Ibid.*, p. xxx.

[17]Babbitt, *Rousseau and Romanticism*, p. 162.

[18]Babbitt, *Democracy and Leadership*, pp. 196-197.

[19] *Ibid.*, pp. 163, 257-258.

[20]Whether Rousseau actually was a primitivist has of course been disputed.

[21]Babbitt, *Rousseau and Romanticism*, p. 44.

[22] *Ibid.*, p. 145; Babbitt, *Democracy and Leadership*, p. 10.

[23]Babbitt, *Literature and the American College*, p. 46.

[24] *Ibid.*, pp. 35-36.

[25] *Ibid.*, p. 69.

[26] *Ibid.*, p. 71.

[27] *Ibid.*, pp. 35-36, 47.

[28] *Ibid.*, pp. 120-121.

[29] *Ibid.*, p. 116.

[30] *Ibid.*

[31] *Ibid.*

[32] *Ibid.*, pp. 108, 163.

[33] *Ibid.*, p. 114.

[34] *Ibid.*, pp. 85, 88-89.

[35] *Ibid.*, p. 90.

[36]See Tate's remarks in C. Hartley Grattan, ed., *The Critique of Humanism* (New York: Brewer and Warren, 1930), p. 150. See also Eliot's remarks in Norman Foerster, ed., *Humanism and America* (New York: Farrar and Rinehart, 1930), pp. 105-113.

[37]Edmund Wilson's reaction is given on page 46, and Malcolm Cowley's reaction on pages 73-75 of Grattan, *The Critique of Humanism*.

[38] *Ibid.*, p. 346.

[39] *Ibid.*, pp. 97-100.

[40] *Ibid.*, p. 23.

[41]For a more extended discussion of the reaction of Roman Catholic intellectuals to Babbitt's views see Louis J. A. Mercier,

The Challenge of Humanism (New York: Oxford University Press, 1933), pp. 177-183.

[42]G. H. Bantock, *Education in an Industrial Society* (London: Faber & Faber, 1963), p. 11.

[43]G. H. Bantock, *Freedom and Authority in Education* (London: Faber & Faber, 1955), pp. 184-185.

[44]Bantock, *Education in an Industrial Society*, pp. 66-67.

[45]*Ibid.*, p. 84.

[46]*Ibid.*, p. 77.

[47]Bantock named these influences in a letter to the writer (August 7, 1974).

[48]Bantock, *Freedom and Authority*, pp. 86-88, 130.

[49]Bantock, *Freedom and Authority*, p. 143. See also G. H. Bantock, *T. S. Eliot and Education* (New York: Random House, 1969), p. 64.

[50]This information was obtained from Bantock's letter to the writer previously mentioned.

[51]G. H. Bantock, *Education, Culture, and the Emotions* (London: Faber & Faber, 1967), pp. 13-14.

[52]Bantock, *Education and Values*, p. 37.

[53]Bantock, *Education, Culture, and the Emotions*, p. 15.

[54]See Bantock's discussion on mental therapy in *ibid.*, pp. 34-35.

[55]The writer of this study based this characterization upon discussions with college faculty members when he was on the admissions and standards committee of a college.

[56]Bantock, *Education and Values*, p. 22.

[57]Bantock, *Education, Culture and the Emotions*, pp. 72-73.

[58]*Ibid.*, pp. 82-83.

[59]Bantock, *Education in an Industrial Society*, pp. 174-175.

[60]For Bantock's views on this subject, see his works, *Education, Culture, and the Emotions*, p. 138, and *Freedom and Authority*, p. 120.

[61] Bantock, *Education, Culture, and the Emotions*, p. 139.

[62]*Ibid.*, p. 140.

[63]Bantock, *Education and Values*, pp. 98-99.

[64]*Ibid.*, p. 100.

[65]Bantock, *Freedom and Authority* p. 198.

66Bantock, *Education in an Industrial Society*, pp. 119-120, 185-186.

67In his book *T. S. Eliot and Education*, Bantock was quite explicit on the importance of early upbringing. See page 111 thereof.

68See the claims made by Carl Bereiter and Siegfried Engelmann, *Teaching Disadvantaged Children in the Preschool* (Englewood Cliffs, New Jersey: Prentice-Hall, 1966), *passim,* and by George Dennison, *The Lives of Children* (New York: Random House, 1969), *passim.* Using diametrically opposite approaches, the authors of both these works claimed considerable success.

69For Bantock's views on the education of the less gifted, see his *Education in an Industrial Society*, pp. 212, 216-220.

70See Bantock's views on Dewey in *ibid.*, pp. 37, 47-48.

71*Ibid.*, p. 199.

72*Ibid.*, pp. 185-186.

73*Ibid.*, pp. 180, 195.

CHAPTER V

THE RELIGIOUS TRADITIONALISM OF BERNARD IDDINGS BELL

An important variant of neo-conservatism will be designated under the rubric of "religious traditionalism" which is most prominently characterized by the view that the fundamental problems of contemporary education are primarily axiological in nature and can only be ultimately solved by adherence to belief in God and in religious values generally.[1] While there is general recognition among neo-conservatives of the value and importance of religion, they have not, on the whole, given it the centrality of position that it occupies in the thinking of the religious traditionalists. For the latter, religious concerns are primary while the aesthetic concerns of the humanists assume only a secondary importance in their minds. A writer who exemplified the religious strain of neo-conservative thought was Canon Bernard Iddings Bell (1886-1958).

An American adherent of High Church Episcopalianism, Canon Bell was ordained into the priesthood in 1910. After serving in a variety of clerical capacities, he became president of St. Stephen's College at the age of thirty-four; serving in that position for fourteen years. When St.

Stephen's was absorbed into Columbia University, he severed his connection due to disagreement with the educational orientation then prevalent at Columbia. From 1930 to 1933, he was however professor of religion at Columbia University. He later was counselor to Episcopal students at the University of Chicago. Subsequently he became blind but continued a productive existence as a canon attached to the Episcopal cathedral of Chicago. During his most productive years, he wrote a considerable number of works on religion and also two books of interest to educators. *Crisis in Education* (1949) pertains to educational problems not only concerning the school but also the home and the church. In *Crowd Culture* (1952), Canon Bell concerned himself with both educational and religious problems.[2]

The primary problem identified by Canon Bell in his educational writings was the immature and emotionally impulsive nature of the American people. To a far greater extent than other peoples and than Americans of an earlier time, the people of the United States suffered from an inversion of values. The primary interest of most Americans was to make money to provide themselves with pleasure and entertainment. Pleasure consisted of enjoying the use of a large and ornate house, a motorcar, expensive clothes, and other material possessions. Entertainment included reading literary "trash" which described acts of brutality and lust as well as listening to or viewing similar material on radio and television. The average American, suffering from religious impoverishment, had long ago lost the concomitant sense of moral dedication which could give life meaning.[3]

If the average American is to obtain happiness, Bell believed that work rather than pleasure must become the center of attention. When pleasure is long pursued, it becomes boring. Unless Americans learn the joys of work, they will "remain petulant children, dangerous, predatory."[4] Work should not be considered an unpleasant burden but rather as an opportunity for creativeness and service to others. Every man is made to give others understanding, tolerance, and clemency. Only through constructive work and moral dedication can men find peace.[5]

According to Bell, that which distinguishes the gentleman from the common man is not money since not all gentlemen are rich nor are all common men poor. What the gentleman has which the common man lacks is a liberal education. By "liberal education," Bell meant an education through which students could learn to discriminate between values and to identify the true ends of living. According to Bell, the common man has received an essentially utilitarian and vocational type of education. As a direct consequent, the common man has shown himself to be incapable of ruling himself or society. Yet, in spite of his evident incapacity to rule, the common man has been given the authority and prerogatives which once belonged to the gentleman.[6] Is it any wonder that the common man is immature? While lacking the wisdom that he might have procured through a liberal education, the common man has responsibilities far exceeding his accomplishments.

If the causes of this inversion of values were believed to be educational, the remedies were also believed to be educational. Bell believed that the major emphasis should be placed on reforming elementary education since, by the time children reached high school, their characters have already been shaped. To accomplish the task of educating the child, the resources not only of the school but also of the home and the church as well should be enlisted. Children should be taught decent manners, the value of craftsmanship, some knowledge of the basic wisdom of the species, religion, and skill in handling the tools of education. Manners were considered important because courtesy was deemed essential to the safety and welfare of civilization.

Manners should be taught primarily in the home but with the assistance of both the church and the school. Craftsmanship was essential to happiness; for to be happy humans must take pride in their work. Craftsmanship would also be taught primarily in the home. Wisdom was needed to enable people to conduct their lives intelligently. Religion was considered to be the essential foundation of morality as well as indispensible if people are to face up to the frustrations of life. Finally, children should learn how to use the educational tools of reading, writing, listening, and speaking if there is to be a competent interchange of ideas.[7]

In general, Bell viewed American problems in fundamentally axiological terms. Americans were emotionally and intellectually immature because they suffered from an inversion of values. The fundamental task of American education was to be a combination of the inculcation of values and of the ability to discriminate between values. The most important function of education was to be the moral one. By this function, Bell meant that through education the individual should learn how to live with himself which knowledge involved learning how to live with others (manners). To learn these things, it was considered necessary that the individual be trained in the nature and application of values. As we shall see later, Bell believed religion to be the indispensable foundation of morality so that ultimately religion was of central importance in Bell's educational philosophy.[8]

The most important trait needed by the student to fulfill his role in Bell's educational plan was intelligence. The term "intelligence" was derived from the words *inter* (between) and *legere* (to choose). Intelligence properly pertained to the ability to discriminate or to differentiate between the permanent and the transitory, the good and the bad, the valuable and the worthless, the beautiful and the ugly.

Intelligence was therefore applicable to intellectual, moral, aesthetic, and prudential judgments.

The possession of high intelligence would not necessarily make the possessor rich, popular, or happy. On the contrary, he might be hated and envied by others. Yet intelligence was essential if proper choices were to be made to enable our civilization to be "safe and free."[9]

While Bell considered intelligence to be basically an innate ability, he believed that education was needed for the full development of this power. While everyone should be taught to discriminate values to the fullest extent to which he or she is capable, it would be unreasonable to expect much from most people. Instead, educators should stress the training and selection of the few who exhibited superior reasoning abilities. From this superior group would come the nation's leaders. According to Bell's conception of intelligence, the elite would be identified by the possession of a considerable degree of analytical and synthetical reasoning abilities—especially with regard to the ability to understand the natures of values and concepts and to discriminate between them. By exposure to a judicious curriculum, characterized by a focus on the liberal arts, the humanities, and religion, those who have the potentialities would presumably be enabled to develop to the point where they would be able to give sapient guidance to the nation. This goal of national service was far more valuable than the treasuring of learning for its own sake which Bell regarded as the dominant goal of American higher education. Bell emphasized ideas rather than facts; reasoning rather than memory.[10]

Bell believed that the most serious deficiency in American life was the absence of any generally accepted ethical standard. American society lacked a generally accepted definition of the nature and purpose of man. Although some theorists might seek to arrive at such a definition by appealing to the will of the majority, Bell rejected this approach as contributing to blind conformity and mediocrity. He also rejected the uncritical acceptance of the traditions of the past as deadly to critical and creative thinking. On the other hand, the rejection of the whole of tradition would lead to foolish behavior. If people are to find meaning in life, they must look to what is beyond man which means that *"religion is involved, primarily involved, inseparably involved in education."*[11]

To Bell, the essence of religion consisted of contact with and adoration of God.[12] Without the foundation of belief in God, morality is liable to degenerate into mere expediency and finally into blind obedience to those who use force.[13] Belief in God is of central importance to moral education. To a considerable extent, moral education is coterminous with religious education.

Bell's view of the nature of religious education was largely based upon Alfred North Whitehead's interpretation of the historical development of the higher religions. According to Bell's account of Whitehead's views, the various religions had originated as rituals which were designed to stimulate emotions that were deemed to be beneficial to the group. Later, people sought to explain rituals in terms of stories. As worshippers continued to perform rituals and to expound the stories linked to their observances, faith was born. When faith was formalized into words, a creed was created. Finally the creed was correlated with other facets of human experience.[14]

Religious instruction should likewise begin with ritual since abstract concepts are too difficult for comprehension by the very young and even by most adults. As soon as the child is old enough, he should learn the stories associated with his religious tradition. When the child reaches the period between ten and fifteen years of age, the ritual should be transformed from a formal into a vital element of his life. By then, the stories would become more significant by being interpreted in the light of the child's growing fund of experience. By insight, the child would become aware of interrelationships between ideas and things that he previously considered separately. Thus faith would emerge. When this stage had been attained, the creed associated with the faith of the child would become meaningful to him.[15]

In the teaching of religion as in the teaching of morals and manners, the home should be the primary focus of learning although there would also exist ancillary activities in both church and school. While considering it neither possible nor necessary to teach the beliefs of any particular denomination in the public schools, Bell believed the respect for the Absolute and some knowledge of the various faiths should be imparted in the classroom. With regard to moral instruction it would be based on "supernatural demands and rest on supernatural sanctions."[16]

Central to Bell's philosophy of religious education was the psychological nature of the child. The particular mode of educational progression was to be from the concrete to the abstract in accordance with the child's growth in experience. In general, Bell believed that people were very flexible by nature. Yet educational content must nevertheless be congruent in content with the native abilities of those being educated. The child should not be introduced to the abstract concepts associated with the various religious creeds until he has matured sufficiently so that he is able to grasp these concepts intelligently. As we have seen, Bell also doubted whether most adults would be able to grasp these concepts fully. Seemingly implicit in this position is the view that heredity is of more importance than the environment in explaining human differences. A staunch environmentalist would be expected to exhibit confidence that under the proper conditions most people would be able to grasp these abstractions.

As to the various levels of formal education, Bell felt that too much time was being spent in schooling children. It seemed to be both wasteful and unreasonable to engage so many people for so long in formal preparation for life. Instead of eight years of elementary education, he recommended a program of six years which would encompass all that was customarily covered in eight. Elementary education would be followed by four years of secondary schooling and three years of college. Graduate or professional training would consume four additional years.[17]

Bell's assumption that an equal amount of formal education is needed for competent performance in all the professions is somewhat surprising considering the great variation existing in the kinds of ability required for success in the various professions. An even more important question is: how would Bell guard against the application of his suggestion for reduction in the length of formal education by administrators to the lowering of academic standards to expand enrollments? To answer this question, Bell's views on educational content at the various levels of instruction will be examined.

Although some attention would be given to content, Bell felt that the basic function of elementary education should be to develop such basic skills as the competency to read, write, speak, listen, compute and handle. The aim of elementary education was thus to develop the basic tools of learning. Bell expressed this position graphically in the following quotation:

"Most Americans cannot read anything more difficult than a picture paper or a pulp magazine; they cannot write a letter and make their meaning plain; they rarely speak except in cliches; they are unable to follow an argument put in the simplest words, to understand what a speaker is driving at. What chance have people to mature when there is no competent interchange of ideas: Our lower schools may be ever so good at conducting classes in 'citizenship' and 'nature study,' though there are those who doubt it when they look at the product; but their main business is and will remain teaching boys and girls how to read, write, speak, listen, figure, and handle things. Unless the lower schools can do a far better job of work on these basic necessities, there will be less and less growing up among Americans."[18]

At the secondary level, Bell recommended additional teaching of the basic skills but on a more advanced level than in the primary grades. Specifically, he wanted a revival of the trivium and the quadrivium for the purpose of inculcating habits of "sound thinking" among the students.[19] In addition to training in the basic skills and the liberal arts, vocational training would be taught in tandem with the liberal arts.[20] In view of his concept of intelligence and his thoughts on the kind of elite that would be best for the nation, it is obvious that Bell held education in the liberal arts in higher esteem than vocational education.

Bell believed that the primary responsibility for the weaknesses of American education rested with the secondary schools. They have failed to provide their students with the basic skills needed for intellectual achievement. Because of the vast numbers of the academically incompetent that yearly enter the secondary schools of the nation, it apparently was decided to lower academic standards to make things easy for the students. The consequence has been a neglect of drill in the basic academic skills. The typical college entrant in the United States was therefore characterized as "mostly an untried young cub" while his counterparts in England and on the European continent were fully prepared for college instruction.[21]

To Bell, the pressure to extend the alleged benefits of

135

mass education to the college level was exceedingly unwise. At the time when he wrote *Crisis in Education*, the colleges were burgeoning with students as a result of the enactment of the "G. I. Bill of Rights." Bell was fearful of the educational consequences of the enactment of this bill. To expand the facilities of the colleges to accommodate a flood of new students would entail an increase in the numbers of faculty and other college personnel far beyond the competently trained supply. Furthermore, concentrating on providing education and facilities for huge masses of students constituted a grave danger that the colleges and universities would neglect the individual student—especially the student of superior academic potential who was precisely the kind of student that Bell thought the colleges should make the center of their attention.[22] His opposition to mass college education was however much broader in scope than his reaction to one congressional bill. As we have seen previously, Bell believed that the chief purpose of higher education should be the training of an elite of ratiocinative intelligence. To admit a mass of poorly prepared students would defeat the main purpose of college and would create an irresistible pressure to lower academic standards and to simplify instruction. To produce a worthy intellectual elite, it was essential that the members of this elite be recruited from those of superior innate intelligence and that those aspiring to membership in the elite be required to survive a challenging program of academic studies.[23]

Bell thought that in college everything should be studied which would throw light on man and his behavior. He specifically mentioned the social sciences, psychology, literature, history, the fine arts, and philosophy. Through the study of these disciplines, it was hoped that the student would learn the causes of human failure and would learn to emulate those human successes worthy of emulation. In essence, Bell valued these disciplines for their value in

136

encouraging students to lead moral and successful lives. Bell's conception of success pertained obviously to happiness rather than money or fame. For him education therefore had essentially practical aims but not in the crass materialistic sense of "practical."[24]

Religion should also be studied on the college level so that the student might come to know and adore the infinite and thereby acquire humility. Bell felt that the student of superior native endowment and education was especially prone to develop the undesirable traits of pride, insolence, and effrontery. Such an individual might have the intellectual qualifications for leadership, but his deficiencies of character would be so serious as to render him positively harmful in any leadership role that he might undertake. To guard against this, it is important that the student learn to look up to what is immeasurably superior to him.[25]

To illustrate what he felt to be important in higher education, Bell recalled that in 1903, when he entered the University of Chicago, he attended an orientation session for incoming freshmen at which the president of the university, Dr. William Rainey Harper, spoke. As Bell recalled it, Dr. Harper said:

"Young gentlemen, you have come here in hope of furthering your education. If you are to do this it would be well for you to have some idea of what an educated human being is. Then you will know what to aim at here, what this institution exists to assist you to become. An educated man is a man who by the time he is twenty-five years old has a clear theory, formed in the light of human experience down the ages of what constitutes a satisying life, a significant life, and who by the age of thirty has a moral philosophy consonant with racial experience. If a man reaches these ages without having arrived at such a theory, such a philosophy, then no matter how many facts he has learned or how many processes he has mastered, that man

137

is an ignoramus and a fool, unhappy, probably dangerous. That is all. Good afternoon."[26]

Bell's conception of higher education embraced study in the liberal arts, the humanities, and religion. In his view, vocational education had no place in the college and the university with the exception of professional study. The fact that he prescribed the same selection of studies for all college students clearly implies that he did not favor reliance upon the elective method of course selection, at least with regard to higher education.

In contrast to Bell's emphasis upon skill instruction in the lower schools, he stressed content quite heavily in his conception of the desirable college curriculum. College courses were not, however, to be taught primarily for their factual content but rather for their value in aiding people to lead happier and more worthy lives. To accomplish this goal, it was necessary to clearly discriminate between values and to know the true ends of living. This view of the purposes of higher education was both moral and intellectual in nature since it involved both the understanding of value concepts and their applications to human conduct.

Bell believed that the chief enemy of education was the state. This menace took the form of a continued attack upon academic freedom to produce conformity so that whichever class happens to be in control shall be kept firmly in power. In the United States, the ruling class was characterized as consisting of "the managerial manipulators for the upper bourgeoisie" and in the future might well include the leaders of organized labor.[27]

The power of the state over education was attributed to the fact that the state was the sole taxing power. This power has resulted in a situation where the state has become the dominant financial entity in education. State control could only expand the tyranny of centralized power. It would be

138

folly to believe it possible for men to wield great power without tyranny as an ultimate consequence.[28]

The significance of Bernard Iddings Bell as an exponent of neo-conservatism can be gauged from the standpoint of the uniqueness of his approach to contemporary educational problems. Unlike other neo-conservative writers, he was not primarily motivated by a feeling of dissatisfaction with the undermining of certain cherished values and practices but rather by the outcomes of this undermining—the production of a population characterized by immaturity and discontent. The remedy lay in an education where the stress would be on the discrimination of purposes and values. Such an educational system would produce an elite capable of leading others to a meaningful existence.

In view of the fact that Bell emphasized moral and especially religious concerns, he would hardly be correctly described as a humanist. The aesthetic and literary aspects of education did not possess for him the dominating importance that they had for genuine humanists. Yet, in spite of these considerations, education was for Bell as for the most intense humanists, primarily a matter of taste. But the tastes that he wished to cultivate were based more fundamentally on religious rather than aesthetic considerations.

In the end, he felt that the meaning of life would be found in happiness. For him, happiness consisted of work—a life of creativity and service to others—buttressed by the emotional security provided by religious faith. In the end, man must find his salvation in religion or not at all.

NOTES

[1]The designation of "religious traditionalism" was chosen because it designates a combination of traditionalist conservatism

139

with religion which, in my view, is eminently descriptive of adherents to this position.

[2]Since the details of Canon Bell's life are not generally known,
the reader is referred to the introduction by Russell Kirk to the
paperback edition of Bernard Iddings Bell, *Crowd Culture*
(Chicago: Henry Regnery Company, 1956), pp. xi-xvi.

[3]On the nature of the American people, see Bernard Iddings
Bell, *Crisis in Education* (New York: Whittlesey House, 1949), pp.
12-24.

[4]*Ibid.*, p. 23.

[5]*Ibid.*, pp. 22-23.

[6]*Ibid.*, pp. 25-26.

[7]*Ibid.*, pp. 31-35.

[8]For Bell's definition of morals and manners, see *ibid.*, p. 83;
with regard to the role of religion, see *ibid.*, pp. 227-228.

[9]*Ibid.*, p. 62.

[10]On the nature and purpose of intelligence, see *ibid.*, pp. 59-
67.

[11]*Ibid.*, p. 228.

[12]*Ibid.*, pp. 127-128.

[13]*Ibid.*, pp. 139-140.

[14]*Ibid.*, pp. 128-130. This reference should be contrasted with
the original account by Alfred North Whitehead, *Religion in the
Making* (New York: Macmillan, 1926) pp. 18, 23. According to
Bell, the four stages of religious development of Whitehead were
ritual, myth, belief, and rationalization. In this characterization,
Bell was in error. Whitehead's stages were ritual, emotion, belief,
and rationalization.

[15]Bell, *Crisis in Education*, pp. 130-135.

[16]*Ibid.*, p. 145. See also *ibid.*, pp. 35, 83.

[17]*Ibid.*, pp. 205-209.

[18]*Ibid.*, pp. 32-33.

[19]*Ibid.*, pp. 70-71.

[20]*Ibid.*, p. 52.

[21]*Ibid.*, p. 47; Bell, *Crowd Culture*, p. 36.

[22]Bell, *Crisis in Education*, pp. 4-5, 65.

[23]*Ibid.*, pp. 66-67.

[24] *Ibid.*, p. 21.
[25] *Ibid.*, p. 72.
[26] *Ibid.*, pp. 57-58.
[27] *Ibid.*, p. 181.
[28] *Ibid.*, pp. 187, 191.

CHAPTER VI

THE NEO-CONSERVATIVE APPROACH TO EDUCATION

Together with the second chapter, which dealt with the philosophical underpinnings of conservatism, the present chapter probably constitutes the most important section of this book. In this chapter, we will analyze and synthesize the thoughts on educational problems of the most influential spokesmen of neo-conservative educational thought to arrive at a comprehensive neo-conservative educational philosophy—characterized by a distinctive approach to educational problems, a theory of learning and an educational methodology. We will also compare our findings with the theoretical inferences which we made in the second chapter. To effectively extrapolate and reconstruct from the writings of the neo-conservatives, we will employ philosophical analysis pertaining to both the basic assumptions and inferences stemming from their viewpoint. We should thereby reach conclusions extending beyond their explicit assertions.

Historically, the conservative metaphysics served as the basic cosmological foundation for the works of such thinkers as Aquinas, Dante, Shakespeare, and Pope. In the sense that these works can never become irrelevant or outdated, conservatism is worth our most serious consideration and attention. Furthermore, neo-conservatism offers to those of us who really desire to improve our society a viable alternative to the dominant educational and social philosophies of today. The educational implications of the neo-conservative viewpoint are therefore of the highest importance. It is the hope of this writer to do justice to this task.

Specifically, the present chapter will be devoted to integration and sharply extending the findings that we have made pertaining to individual neo-conservative writers for the purpose of uncovering the basic educational characteristics and implications of the neo-conservative movement. We will begin by summarizing our findings pertaining to historical influences upon neo-conservative educational thought. We will then consider in order the general aims and content of education; methods of instruction and learning theory; and the agencies that should be involved in the educational process. A comparison will then be made with the inferences made in the second chapter and then certain general conclusions will be reached. In essence, this chapter will be devoted to an attempt to piece together the outlines of a neo-conservative educational philosophy based upon the philosophical analysis of actual empirical evidence.

Neo-conservative educational thought derived many of its characteristics from the historical period in which it flourished. The contemporary period, which in its essential intellectual characteristics began shortly after World War I, represents an advanced stage in the decline of traditional moral and cultural standards. Without exception, the neo-conservative writers discussed in this study have viewed the problems of the contemporary age as being fundamentally axiological in character. They have protested against a condition which they have seen as arising from a combination of a lack of standards in some areas of endeavor and an inversion of standards in other areas. Two trends have been particularly disturbing to neo-conservatives: the decline of faith in objective moral standards and the spread of cultural and educational equalitarianism. From the neo-conservative perspective, the rejection of objective moral standards was a symptom of the general decline of standards; equalitarianism was a result of this inversion of standards. To restore a climate of intellectual and moral integrity, neo-conservatives advocated a reversal of these trends. The primary means to be employed was to be educational in character.

Contrary to popular opinion, the writing of Edmund Burke was not the primary source of inspiration of neo-conservative educational thought. Of the writers surveyed, we have sufficient data to reach conclusions on the sources of inspiration of all of them with the exception of Bernard Iddings Bell. These writers include what are almost certainly the three most frequently mentioned neo-conservative writers in the American and British literature on conservatism—Babbitt, Eliot, and Kirk. Of the writers surveyed, only Russell Kirk looked to Edmund Burke as his chief inspiration. The influences upon the other writers, including Babbitt, Bantock, and Eliot, were so varied as to discourage meaningful generalizations beyond the bare fact that these influences were chiefly conservative in nature. While neo-conservative writers on education agreed in a general way with many of the views of Edmund Burke, they apparently did not as a group derive most of their views directly from his writings.

A more fruitful means of ascertaining the historical influences upon the neo-conservatives would be to compare their views with those of the various preceding schools of educational thought. From this historical perspective, contemporary conservative educational thought has been predominantly humanistic in nature.[1] With the exception of Bell, the writers surveyed exhibited the aesthetic emphasis characteristic of humanism. All of these writers shared a common emphasis upon the study of literature. In addition, Babbitt, Bantock, and Kirk also believed in the superior efficacy of insight—an ability which was based to a considerable degree on the imagination, a faculty commonly stressed by humanists. Since T. S. Eliot was an imaginative poet, it is probable that he too believed in the importance of insight even though he was not very explicit on this matter in his educational writings. Furthermore, both Babbitt and Eliot stressed the aesthetical ideals of harmony and proportion. Babbitt, Eliot, and Kirk also exhibited a common emphasis upon classical Greco-Roman literature.

In general, neo-conservative thought should be viewed as an outgrowth of a tradition which began with the aesthetic aspects of the philosophies of Plato and Aristotle and was further developed through the work of such figures as Isocrates, Cicero, Quintilian, John of Salisbury, and numerous Renaissance personalities. In addition, several neo-conservative writers, especially Bell and Eliot, were also strongly influenced by Christian ideals. In historical perspective, neo-conservatism, at least in its educational aspects, should be considered a reaction against contemporary nihilism and equalitarianism in favor of an emphasis upon humanistic and sometimes Christian ideals. *On the whole, neo-conservatism represents an elitist form of humanism.*

The particular values which neo-conservatives have stressed were moral, intellectual, and religious in character. Economic values and those values pertaining to physical comfort and sociability were generally ignored. *On the whole, as was demonstrated in the second chapter, there is implicit in conservative metaphysics, a structural-functional axiology with prime importance being given to speculative wisdom sometimes*

146

combined with beatitude or the mystical experience of union with the Divine. Neo-conservative writers were generally not very explicit in this regard but, as we pointed out much earlier in this study, such an axiology is most consistent with conservative metaphysical premises and has in the remote past, been closely associated with conservative ideology.

To neo-conservatives, the meaning of life tends to lie in growth and achievement. To that end, the neo-conservatives were quite willing to sacrifice a considerable degree of psychological freedom in favor of the restraints and discipline which they felt to be necessary for significant achievement. In general, they espoused an ethical perfectionism with emphasis upon spiritual or non-material aspects of human endeavor. *This perfectionism was to be measured in terms of the development of the individual rather than the uplift of society.* The various values espoused by conservatives can be linked together through the implicit ideal of the highly cultivated gentleman. This ideal is in accord with the basic humanistic virtues of harmony and proportion; for the discretion and general restraint of the gentleman are obviously conducive to harmony, and the good taste which he is supposed to manifest includes the ability to perceive what is proportionate and harmonious.

The fundamental aim of education as perceived by neo-conservatives was the development of an elite characterized by the ability to discriminate between ideas and values in terms of their intrinsic nature and relative worth. Education thus becomes a matter of taste. Notice what is involved in this conception of education. It becomes the primary task of the educator to model the cognitive processes of his charges after the universal hierarchical model which underlies conservative ontology and axiology. This implies a stress on general academic education for the purpose of training the individual in certain basic intellectual and aesthetic ideas and values deemed to be of universal worth. Furthermore, the training

147

of leadership was deemed to be more important than the uplift of the masses. In particular, the neo-conservatives strove for an elite possessed of a high degree of ratiocinative intelligence so that they might be able to interrelate general concepts. Therefore, the emphasis must be on those subjects, such as the humanities and the social sciences, which are most concerned with ideas and values.

Admission to higher schools would be based upon evidences of one's competency to profit from such an experience. As a group, neo-conservatives felt that the ratiocinative potentialities of the vast majority of people were very limited. For this reason, the neo-conservatives advocated selective education on the college and university level. *They generally felt that mass higher education would inevitably lead to the lowering of educational standards since colleges would be subjected to pressures to simplify instruction and to expand their facilities far beyond the limits that could be considered qualitatively desirable.* These outcomes would inevitably deflect colleges from the task of developing the intelligent and discriminating student body which might form the basis of a cultivated national leadership.

To fully grasp what is really at issue in this regard, it is helpful to survey the arguments that have been employed by the advocates of mass higher education. These arguments have generally been based on grounds of either individual excellence or of good citizenship. On individual grounds, mass higher education was justified as enabling people to improve their abilities, to enhance their occupational efficiency, and to lead happier lives. On political grounds, mass education was deemed to be essential to enable the electorate to exercise the duties of citizenship intelligently.[2] For example, the President's Commission on Higher Education, 1947-1948, used both the individual and political arguments to recommend that American college courses be made less verbal and less intellectual in order to bring them within the range of more people.³ To a conservative, this recommendation is a clear illustration of how the advocacy of mass education can lead to a demand for the lowering of standards. Of course, it is doubtful whether the members of the President's Commission would concur with the view that their recommendation would lead to a lowering of standards.

The crux of the controversy between the advocates of selective education and the partisans of mass higher education pertains to the capability of the masses of people to grasp or comprehend. The benefits cited by the proponents of mass education could not, for the most part, be obtained unless the students themselves possessed the ability to understand and utilize the knowledge conveyed by their professors. The neo-conservatives have evinced a lack of confidence in the ability of the majority to clearly grasp in all its significance the abstract conceptual knowledge deemed essential for responsible leadership. As we have seen, the conservative criterion of academic competence pertained primarily to the ability to analyze and to interrelate general concepts. *In other words, neo-conservatives regard a good student as one who can comprehend the pattern of abstract concepts in relationship to one another.* Academic achievement is not simply a matter of absorbing information but rather of structuring knowledge; to neo-conservatives, information is not true knowledge unless it has been integrated with other information into a patterned structure so that interrelationships are apparent. Neo-conservatives have thus been skeptical of the efficacy of attempting to instruct individuals who have evinced little interest and competence in academic areas. This skepticism seems based on the assumption that heredity or early upbringing are more important than education and other environmental factors in explaining the academic competencies of students. Had the neo-conservatives conceived of education in terms of the passive absorption of

149

knowledge rather than of understanding and structuring it, they might well have been more sanguine concerning the potentialities of students since the mere learning of isolated facts is probably easier than the integration of those facts into a meaningful whole. Opponents of educational conservatism have not all necessarily conceived of education in strictly factual terms, but they have generally stressed the role of the environment in explaining human differences.

The advocates and opponents of selectivity in higher education disagree on what should be the primary focus of education on the college level. The opponents of selection are concerned with the uplift of the vast majority of students while the proponents of selection desire to devote their efforts to those who exhibit the greatest intellectual potentiality. When the President's Commission on Higher Education recommended that higher education be made less verbal and less intellectual, it revealed a propensity to adapt the nature of higher education to make it available to more people.[4] It is highly probable that some of the members of this group had implicitly assumed that the common welfare depended more on raising the average level of academic attainment than on the development of competent leadership. On the other hand, the neo-conservatives assumed that the welfare of the nation depended more on the development of an elite of wisdom and character. One of the causes for this disagreement pertained to a difference of opinion concerning the academic potentialities of the majority of students. Another basis for disagreement might well have been a difference of historical interpretation concerning the importance of leadership in contrast to the power of mass movements in shaping the course of history.

Neo-conservatives generally emphasized the transmission of the wisdom of the past to present and future generations. Implicit in this emphasis was the assumption of the existence of certain verities which would not alter with time. In contrast to John Dewey and other pragmatist educators, the neo-conservatives did not stress change but rather focused on what they regarded as eternal values.

The neo-conservatives have generally maintained that tradition is an efficacious and worthwhile vehicle for the transmission of values since it contains the funded wisdom of the past. *In contrast to those writers, such as Hutchins and Adler, who have advocated only the imparting of the wisdom of the famous, the neo-conservatives have also stressed the transmission of the values of the various folk cultures of the world.* Certain neo-conservatives, such as T. S. Eliot and Russell Kirk, have emphasized the importance of tradition as a remedy for some of the ills of the twentieth century; other neo-conservatives, such as Irving Babbitt and G. H. Bantock, have evinced less optimism concerning the practicality of tradition as an answer for contemporary ills.

Concerning the content of education, the neo-conservatives have all stressed the importance of the liberal arts. Literature was especially emphasized; especially as a means whereby students might learn the nature and applications of ethical values. Of the two qualities most emphasized by conservatives, wisdom and virtue, virtue was generally held to be primary. *By focusing on literature as the major avenue of moral instruction, neo-conservatives implicitly relied upon concrete situations rather than abstract principles as the preferred method of approach.* Their method therefore tended to be more inductive than deductive. One exception to the general stress on the literary method of value instruction was Bernard Iddings Bell who espoused a fundamentally religious approach.

As a group, the neo-conservatives preferred a prescribed curriculum to the elective principle of course selection. The most prevalent reasons for opposing the elective principle

151

were that young people lacked the needed competences for making sensible selections and that studies differed from one another in intrinsic value. Conservatives preferred to prescribe subjects on a hierarchical basis with those believed to embody spiritual (moral, religious, and intellectual) values placed at the summit. In contrast, the widely known defense of the elective principle by Charles W. Eliot, former president of Harvard University, might be cited. Eliot was confident that all studies if pursued with vigor and efficiency would be of equal value. Motivation was deemed to be important in determining how efficiently studies would be pursued. He therefore felt that students should have the opportunity to study the subjects of greatest interest to them. He was confident that the mature student could make wise choices.

In general, the neo-conservatives did not stress the factor of interest. They believed it to be more important to choose subjects of high intrinsic worth than to minister to the fickle desires of the students. They were not very confident of the competency of even mature students nor of the purity of their motives when choosing subjects. Irving Babbitt exemplified this skepticism when he suspected that indolence might prove to be more important than interest as a determining factor in the choice of electives. The neo-conservative attitude toward the elective principle resembled their view of mass higher education. On both issues, a strong consciousness of human limitations was manifested.

The neo-conservatives expressed some interesting views on teaching methods although not in as great detail as we might like. Since instructional procedures are ultimately based upon learning theories, we should inquire into the learning theory which underlies neo-conservative educational philosophy, if we are to obtain a clear idea of their educational methodology. Since none of the neo-conservative writers considered was an educational psychologist, it is hardly surprising that no one of these writers has expounded a systematic theory of learning. We do however have certain indications of their fundamental attitudes and from these instances should be able to extrapolate the outlines of a learning theory.

To this writer, the most striking fact about neo-conservative views concerning learning is their strong resemblance to Gestalt psychology.[5] Like the Gestalt psychologists, the neo-conservatives have considered learning to be primarily an interactive process in which both the teacher and the student play significant roles. In agreement with the conservative principle of respect for authority, neo-conservatives have stressed the role of the teacher as leader and guide in the classroom. In addition, the neo-conservatives have also stressed the importance of considering the abilities of the child. The teacher should therefore modify his own lesson plans to suit the nature of the students in front of him.[6]

Like the Gestalt psychologists, the neo-conservatives also stress the importance of insight. With the exception of T. S. Eliot, all the neo-conservatives considered in this study underscored the educational importance of insight whether they termed it the "illative sense," "seeing patterns," or simply "intuition." Generally they conceived of insight as the power to integrate separate details into meaningful wholes. Insight was generally deemed to be the product of a combination of the faculties of the imagination and reason although Kirk, following Newman, included other faculties as well. Generally, reason was to act as the final judge of the generalties arrived at by the use of the imagination. Of particular concern to the neo-conservatives was the utilization of insight to abstract and interrelate general ideas and values.

What method should a teacher employ to teach insightfully? Although the neo-conservatives have not been very explicit in this regard, enough experiments have been performed by Gestalt psychologists to give us important clues.[7]

Since insight occurs largely in the mind of the student, it would seem to be obvious that the teacher would have to rely on the discussion method rather than on giving answers to the student. *It is important that the discussion take place in a structured situation where the teacher leads the student sequentially to the attainment of the insight that the teacher wishes to convey.* This sequential procedure would presumably start with a review of all relevant material because insight is fundamentally the power to integrate what has been learned into a structured whole. The teacher should then ask the student questions designed to focus attention on those aspects of the whole which are relevant to the attainment of the desired insight. The Socratic method is a fine example of such a form of questioning.

To neo-conservatives, learning at its best pertained to understandings more than to facts. The basic academic skills were to be acquired in the lower schools in preparation for the integrated understandings to be obtained in colleges. The emphasis was therefore on the content of learning. Techniques were deemed important primarily as instruments for the acquisition of the understandings. In this respect, they differed significantly from the mental disciplinarians who stressed learning skills more than content and from the educational realists who placed greater stress on factual information.

To achieve their aims, the neo-conservatives had to stress a basically academic type of instruction since they were concerned largely with ideas and values although they were, as we have seen, ready to use aesthetic and affective approaches for their cognitive values. As for those students who have not exhibited noticeable academic talent, most neo-conservatives recommended that after they have acquired enough formal education to function usefully in the non-academic world, they should be encouraged to pursue their further education through practical experience. Ban-

154

tock differed in this respect from the others in that he had greater confidence that the students would benefit from further formal instruction although of a practical rather than academic character. Nevertheless, neo-conservatives as a whole stressed the importance of human differences when planning learning procedures and programs.

Concerning the agencies to be employed in the educational process, there was general agreement that while the major function of the school should be educational, other institutions should also play their roles. The family was especially emphasized as an agency ideally suited for instruction in morals, manners, and the cultural traditions of society. The church was also deemed important for supplying the religious instruction so strongly emphasized by the neo-conservative writers including even the skeptic, Irving Babbitt.[8] They were also concerned about the educational effects of printed materials, paintings, and musical compositions. The concern was especially evident in the writings of Eliot and Bell but was to some extent true of all the writers under discussion. Although the school was considered to be the primary agency of formal education, other institutions were also therefore deemed to be important. As proponents of traditionalism, conservative writers would be expected to stress the educational significance of those institutions which have been the primary conduits of tradition—especially the family and the church. In this respect, the neo-conservatives were simply being consistent with their basic assumptions.

In the second chapter, the basic philosophical presuppositions of neo-conservatism were uncovered and certain implications were inferred. On the whole, the neo-conservatives have fulfilled our expectations regarding the educational entailments of the conservative viewpoint. They have however neglected one major area. Our inferences pertaining to the approach of the conservative school counselor have not been confirmed because the neo-conservatives have largely neglected the entire area of school counseling. Yet it is undeniable that this is an important area of educational endeavor. By the study of neo-conservative implications concerning school counseling, we can infer the general neo-conservative attitude on the nature of the individual student and his fundamental needs; for the counselor is concerned with the personal desires and problems of the student.

As was pointed out in the second chapter, the conservative view of human nature has been characterized by a stress on the weakness and irrationality of mankind. *Humans were not depicted as free and autonomous but as continually beset by anxieties.* The needs for security, status, and meaning were considered especially strong. Most of these needs could only be satisfied by the establishment of satisfactory relationships between the individual and society. These anxieties have multiplied during the twentieth century by the steady undermining of the traditional institutions of society. Neo-conservatives have especially concerned themselves with the erosion of belief in traditional standards of value and with the rising tide of equalitarianism.

These views obviously have many implications pertaining to school counseling. In accordance with conservative presuppositions, as we have seen in the second chapter of this study, the conservative counselor should be concerned with helping students to develop a meaningful philosophy of life. This attitude is consonant with the neo-conservative stress on the meanings and discrimination of values.

The conservative counselor should also be concerned with helping the student to find his proper niche in the vocational, intellectual, and social hierarchies. To do this efficiently, the counselor should help the student to ascertain his vocational and educational assets and limitations including a realistic understanding of what goals the student should sensibly strive to achieve. *In this respect, the conservative counselor would stand in sharp contrast to his more equalitarian counterparts whose confidence in the efficacy of environmental influences would make them more responsive to the desires of the student than to his manifested capabilities.* If, for example, a student expresses interest in a profession apparently unsuited to his abilities, the more equalitarian type of counselor would presumably be inclined to try to overcome the deficiencies of the student while the conservative would be more likely to suggest that the student change his goal. This difference in approach is obviously based on a difference in the estimation of the efficacy of environmental influences.

In view of the importance that neo-conservatives have imputed to the social relationships of the individual, the conservative counselor should seek to involve students in cooperative social endeavor as a means of relieving the anxieties that periodically trouble people. This should not be interpreted as implying that the conservative would necessarily prefer cooperation to competition. The strong achievement of conservatives would militate against the indiscriminate acceptance of cooperation as a desirable value; *for the conservative stress on selective excellence entails a certain amount of competition if selectivity is to be effective.* Other things being equal, whether competition or cooperation is to be acceptable would presumably depend upon which practice in a given situation would most enhance achievement.

The values which the conservative school counselor would seek to effectuate would presumably not be permissive in nature but would include the hardier virtues which have figured so prominently in conservative educational thought such as discipline and restraint. *The conservative view of happiness has not been couched in terms of relaxation and pleasure but rather in terms of challenge and vigorous response.*

157

Yet the conservative ideal of happiness has not been completely individualistic in character; for while the individual must strive by himself to achieve, he is also in need of sociability with other members of his species. Above all, the individual needs a coherent, integrated philosophy of life.

The greatest deficiencies of neo-conservative educational thought are probably the absence of a systematic analysis of the educational dimensions of neo-conservatism and the absence of speculation on the implications of neo-conservatism pertaining to guidance and counseling. It is hoped that this study will contribute toward alleviating these deficiencies.

The greatest deficiency of neo-conservatism as a general philosophical system is probably the absence of a detailed integration of conservative metaphysics with the findings of modern science; especially concerning the concept of hierarchy. The importance of this task is obvious; for the conservative remedy for the perplexities of the contemporary age may in the last analysis be the truly viable one. This remedy would consist in short of an emphasis on a structural-functional system of objective values together with insistence upon a life of vigorous and rigorous achievement. The conservative answer to the anxieties of the present lies to a considerable extent in striving for a worthwhile future. This is truly a Promethean ideal of life. Perhaps this is what the West needs.

NOTES

[1] For the sense in which we are employing the term "humanism" see pages 51-52 of this study.

[2] For arguments in favor of mass higher education see Gail

Kennedy, ed., *Education for Democracy* (Boston: Heath, 1952), pp. 78-80.

³The Kennedy anthology contains, among other selections, the findings of the President's Commission. For pertinent passages see especially pp. 8, 13.

⁴*Ibid.*, p. 13.

⁵For a general explication of Gestalt learning theory see Morris L. Bigge, *Learning Theories for Teachers* (New York: Harper and Row, 1964), pp. 278-285.

⁶The view of Gestalt psychologists regarding the role of students was similar to that of the neo-conservatives. The former tended however to view teachers more as guides than leaders. See *ibid.* for more details.

⁷*Ibid.* The Gestalt psychologists were of course not necessarily conservative themselves but they shared the conservative's stress on insight.

⁸See page 97 of this study.

CHAPTER VII

REFLECTIONS ON THE ROLE OF NEO-CONSERVATISM IN AMERICAN EDUCATION

A useful means of assessing the significance of neo-conservatism in American education would be to compare neo-conservatism with related educational philosophies. The conventional textbook treatment of educational philosophies embodies a division of the right-wing of educational thought into the perennialist and essentialist approaches. In common with neo-conservatives, the adherents of both these educational viewpoints stress academic education in contrast to those who prize social adjustment, vocational training, and athletics. They also advocate a structured organized classroom situation with the teacher in the role of authority, and they are all inclined to be skeptical of the efficacy of the elective principle in determining curriculum content. In contrast, their opponents on the educational Center and Left place greater stress on freedom for the student and on a broader, more ambitious program of educational services.

The split between the perennialists and the essentialists is conventionally attributed to a difference of emphasis pertaining to curriculum content. Perennialists stress the study of the great classics of the past—either in accordance with conventional subject-matter categories or in terms of the great books courses. The essentialists, on the other hand, focus on those studies which would give students the *skills* needed to function well in the contemporary world. In other words, perennialists emphasize content while essentialists emphasize skills. The basic contrast will be further clarified by a more detailed examination of each of these two philosophies.

As a distinct school of educational thought, perennialism achieved importance in the nineteen-thirties. It represented an effort to provide a coherent and integrated philosophy of life in response to the onslaught upon the traditional verities of the relativists and the skeptics. The remedies suggested by the perennialists revolved around the study and the intelligent appreciation of the classics of the past—especially those relating to the humanities and the social sciences. Among the influential figures associated with this movement were Mortimer J. Adler, Robert M. Hutchins, and Mark Van Doren.

In common with Aristotle, the perennialists emphasized the development and cultivation of human reason. The intellectual values were especially stressed as being intrinsically good in themselves although those perennialists strongly influenced by St. Thomas Aquinas ranked the religious values above the intellectual. The perennialists assumed both the existence and knowability of absolute standards of value. They also assumed the intrinsic superiority of the classics to other works of literature.

As we have previously noted, the perennialists combined these views with adherence to the democratic rhetoric popular among Americans. The perennialist hostility to aristocratic and elitist views was often quite vigorous, such as Hutchins' famous exchange with T. S. Eliot referred to in the fourth chapter of this study. Liberal education was deemed to be practicable for mass consumption. Even when selective education was advocated, this was usually done with reluctance and not to recruit an intellectual, business, or political elite.

Perennialists have been split into neo-rationalist and neo-Thomist wings. Neo-rationalists were generally thought of as followers of Aristotle—especially with regard to his stress upon reason. The neo-Thomists would adhere to Aristotelian rationalism but would add to this the reliance upon faith of St. Thomas Aquinas.

Actually, this distinction has been exaggerated. It is a well known fact that many of the leading neo-rationalists such as Adler and Hutchins have been strongly influenced by St. Thomas Aquinas. Furthermore, the neo-Thomists represent a wide variety of educational views ranging from those of Father William McGucken to the more liberal views of Jacques Maritain. There is however an obvious perennialist aspect common to all forms of neo-Thomistic educational thought.

Perennialists have much in common with neo-conservatives; for there is a perennialist aspect to neo-conservative thought as well. There are, however, two noteworthy differences. The perennialist adherence to tradition is generally confined to the more consciously intellectual and aesthetic aspects thereof. They view their traditional heritage in terms of the "great" books and other cultural creations of the past. They neglect the traditions embodied in the various folk cultures while the transmission of the folkways and mores associated with the societies in which they live is a concern for neo-conservatives for this is in accordance with the fundamental values which define conservatism *per se*. Secondly, perennialists adhere generally to a democratic rhetoric; neo-conservatives, to an aristocratic rhetoric. The problem of the recruitment of a superior quality of leadership assumes an importance in neo-conservative literature which is not matched in perennialist literature. The latter are generally more hopeful concerning the innate potentialities of the general run of students.

Such differences stem from differences in the intrinsic natures of the two philosophies. The perennialists were, as we have just seen, primarily influenced by the rationalistic aspects of Aristotelianism while the predominant historical influence upon neo-conservative educational thought was classical humanism. Rationalists *per se* are inclined to place less stress on folk traditions than humanists—for these traditions are generally transmitted intuitively and by imitation rather than through processes of conscious ratiocination. Furthermore, in the history of the Western world, humanism has, until recently, been closely associated with an aristocratic conception of education. While there was certainly an aristocratic strain in the philosophy of Aristotle, it has certainly not been stressed by the perennialists. These historical differences also explain the contrast between the philosophical emphasis of the perennialists and the literary emphasis of most neo-conservative writers on education.

Essentialism was embodied in the works of such individuals as William C. Bagley, Arthur E. Bestor, Jr., and Henry E. Morrison. In general, essentialists believe that there are certain subjects which should be studied by all students if they are to function with maximum efficiency in society. These include such tool subjects as reading, writing, arithmetic, spelling, and composition. Mastery of these subjects would be needed to provide the basic skills with which to pursue learning. Following the study of these subjects in elementary school, students are to pursue the study of fundamental content subjects on the secondary school level. The latter include such disciplines as geography, history, mathematics, sciences, literature, and languages. The mastery of these subjects would in turn provide students with the wherewithal to pursue the same disciplines on a more advanced level and to add other subjects as well. The pursuit of these studies was generally justified in utilitarian terms; that they prepare students to function well as workers and citizens and contribute to the welfare of society.

Essentialists therefore stress the mastery of primarily academic skills pursued in terms of conventional subject matter parameters. The basic function of the school is therefore deemed to be academic in nature. Although some essentialists would add vocational and social functions to the list of school services, there is a marked tendency among essentialists to view such functions with misgivings; for they suspect that the assumption of such services by the schools undermines the essential function of providing academic skills and understandings.

In contrast to the perennialists, essentialists focus on matters of contemporary concern rather than on transmitting the values of the past. Essentialists are not *necessarily* hostile to the heritage of the past; it simply is not at the center of their attention. In fact, the leaders of the essentialist movement tend to approach problems from a non-traditionalist and rarely even an anti-traditionalist standpoint. In common with the perennialists, the essentialists, however, do combine a dedication to academic concerns with an essentially democratic, rather than aristocratic, approach. In general, the perennialists concern themselves primarily with values; the essentialists, with functions.

Essentialism has often been divided into idealistic and realistic wings in accordance with differences in epistemology and metaphysics. The idealists view the universe as basically mental or spiritual in nature while realists feel that the actual world is similar to what is disclosed by our senses. The former therefore stress ideas and values; the latter, facts. In this writer's view, the classification of educational

165

idealism as a species of essentialism is questionable; for idealists do not exhibit the utilitarianism so characteristic of essentialists as a group but instead concern themselves with the perfection of the individual in imitation of the Absolute. The fact that most of them do not focus on the classics of the past is not in my opinion sufficient warrant for placing them under the essentialist rubric.

As we have noticed before, there was a strong tendency of both the essentialists and perennialists to combine the advocacy of an academic liberal arts type of education with a democratic rhetoric manifested chiefly in the form of an essential distrust of aristocratic and elitist approaches to education. In this respect, neo-conservatives differ decisively from their allies on the educational Right.

In other respects, the essentialists contrast more sharply with the neo-conservatives than do the perennialists; for while the perennialists espouse a kind of traditionalism by their emphasis upon the classics, the essentialists fail to exhibit traditionalism in either of the senses commonly employed by conservatives—an emphasis upon the classics and/or the heritage of the various folk cultures of the world. Furthermore, the utilitarianism of the essentialists contrasts markedly with the axiological emphasis of both the perennialists and the neo-conservatives. *If educational writers had confused neo-conservatism with perennialism, it would be much more understandable than their widespread confusion of neo-conservatism with essentialism.*

Up to now, the focus of this study has been primarily on the analysis and relationships of neo-conservatism as a philosophy and as an educational movement. To ascertain the essential significance of educational neo-conservatism in the world today, we must now seek to *evaluate* it in relationship to current tendencies and trends. To do so effectively, it is essential to become more subjective in our essential approach. In the writer's opinion, the primary contribution that neo-conservatives can make to the nation today is as a much needed corrective to certain trends in American education and in the larger context of American society as a whole. Since current American social trends are reflected, albeit in more moderate terms, throughout the Western world, what neo-conservatives have to say about these problems obviously has more than merely national significance. Let us therefore discuss the points that are particularly relevant to contempoary concerns.

First of all, the conservative stress on restraint rather than permissiveness is greatly needed to restore the balance at a time when the emphasis upon permissiveness has become more and more pronounced. It is a commonplace that American education and American society as a whole has been marked by a much more libertarian approach than their European counterparts. Neo-conservatism can perform a much-needed function in helping to bring about a more balanced attitude toward the problem of freedom versus restraint. The soaring crime rate and the decline of those public civilities that are supposed to characterize a highly civilized society should be stark reminders that the balance has indeed been grievously upset.

The neo-conservatives have, in this writer's opinion, sensibly recognized that if restraints are to be meaningful, they must be applied judiciously and in accordance with recognized standards of value. For decades, college students have been encouraged to view human behavior relativistically; so that they would understand rather than evaluate this behavior in the light of their own experiences. After the atrocities committed by the Hitlerites, many American intellectuals realized that their consciences have been offended by these acts but that their own relativistic principles left them powerless to express their moral indignation in intellectually acceptable terms. Especially to be feared is the rise of a new generation which would be rendered morally insensitive by adherence to ethical and cultural relativism. The neo-conservative advocacy of a reaffirmation of traditional standards therefore seems to this writer to be very timely. Their emphasis on the central importance of conveying a standard of values and a metaphysics which would serve as a foundation for such a standard is very appropriate at this time of history.

The neo-conservatives have generally not been very explicit concerning the particular value standards to be applied. There is however, a severe need for the detailed analysis of the structure of values. In the second chapter, the outlines were set forth of such a value structure which was based on the same hierarchical Aristotelian viewpoint which historically has served as the foundation for conservative metaphysics. The approach was in essence to grasp the natures of values in terms of the functions which these values were assumed to serve. The moral virtues would be graded on a scale in terms of the degree of self-control required; just acts, in terms of the degree of proportionateness; intellectual virtues, in terms of which virtues guide the exercise of the others. The virtues as a whole would then be graded in terms of their closeness to speculative wisdom to which some thinkers would add either beatitude or mystical union on the grounds that ideally the exercise of these virtues would determine how the other virtues would be expressed. In effect, this is a teleological means-ends network which culminates in an end such as speculative wisdom or mystical union which is intrinsically valuable—not simply a means to the attainment of another value. The three figures who have doubtless most influenced neo-conservative thinking on values—Aristotle, Plato, and St. Thomas Aquinas—have adhered to systems of value substantially similar to this one. This entire structural functional methodology for the ranking of values is based upon the assumption of the objective reality of values regardless of whether these values are conceived of as imminent in the universe, as in the case of Aristotle, or transcendent over the temporal world, as in the case of Plato. Another assumption basic to this entire conception is that each value has an essential function in the universe which is determined by the very nature of that value—regardless of how humans may choose to utilize them. Thus, individual persons might choose to utilize wisdom not as an intrinsic good but rather as a means of procuring fame and fortune. Such a point of view would be viewed by the savants concerned as an inversion of standards. Wisdom should guide desire— not desire, wisdom. To think otherwise is to place the evanescent above the eternal.

These considerations should bring us inevitably to what the neo-conservatives have regarded as one of the central problems of democratic government—the recruitment of a leadership characterized by wisdom and moral virtue. The political scandals of the last few years have brought this problem to the public with a forcefulness which has probably been greater than ever before in American history. The cures suggested by journalists and politicians, such as the tightening of regulations governing campaign spending and the public disclosure of campaign contributions, hardly touch the root of the problem. As we have seen, neo-conservatives were concerned about this problem long before the so-called Watergate scandals. In their view, the problem is fundamentally educational in nature. How can we hope to procure leadership of quality when our educational system has been so strongly geared to mediocrity? To recruit a political leadership of which we can be proud, we need to inculcate in the people an appreciation of those qualities which comprise what we mean by excellence. Neo-conservatives have felt that American higher education should follow the example of some other countries and make the training of leadership of all sorts—political,

169

economic, intellectual, artistic, etc., etc., its central concern. There should be an insistence upon high standards of academic achievement without compromise in the awarding of the various academic distinctions. The primary standard of judgment would be, as we have seen many times in this book, ratiocinative ability or the capacity to understand and see the relationships between universal concepts. Implicit in this entire position is the replacement of so-called practical considerations by professional standards of educational conduct. Such a change would give the educational profession the dignity it deserves.

In this era, when we hear of students graduating high school who can neither read nor write and when we hear of others who are functional illiterates, the neo-conservative concern for academic excellence should find a sympathetic hearing among American parents and taxpayers who have time and again exhibited serious misgivings over the quality of American education.

The neo-conservative emphasis upon the humanities and the social sciences can serve as a needed corrective to the excessive concentration upon commercial and technological training that has been characteristic of American education. The United States has achieved considerable eminence in scientific and technological fields though scientists of foreign birth and training have contributed considerably to this reputation. American standing in the humanities and the social sciences has not been on a par. Yet if scientific discoveries are to be used wisely, there should be some attention given to the ethical, religious, and sociological implications of scientific advances. In addition, as conservatives have so often pointed out, education in the liberal arts is intrinsically as well as instrumentally valuable.

If we compare neo-conservatism with essentialism and perennialism, we find that all three wings of the educational Right have exhibited an emphasis upon restraints rather than permissiveness in education and a stress upon the academic form of education although essentialists tend to justify this view on utilitarian grounds rather than in terms of the intrinsic worth of this type of education. In addition, the perennialists, like the neo-conservatives, stress the need for the inculcation of objective standards of value as guides to students in developing themselves and in pursuing their life activities.

Neither essentialists nor perennialists have on the whole stressed the importance of qualitative excellence nor have they exhibited the same consciousness of the problem of leadership that has been characteristic of the neo-conservatives. The democratic rhetoric characteristic of the exponents of both essentialism and perennialism is indicative of their lack of realization of something of which neo-conservatives have been acutely conscious—that the democratic concern for the majority must be moderated by a sense of selective excellence if democratic education and government are to work well. Particularly to be guarded against is the inveterate American hostility to elites. This has not resulted in the disappearance of an American elite but rather too often in the presence of an elite recruited by haphazard methods because Americans could not psychologically accept the idea of any formal means of elite recruitment. Provided that everyone has the opportunity to compete on the basis of his own individual qualities for membership in the elite, regardless of race, social class, or economic status, there can be no validity to the objection that such selection is unfair. A consciously selected elite would almost certainly raise the general level of American leadership—which, especially in the political sphere, often requires great wealth for success. In this respect, the United States is certainly more undemocratic than some European nations. The conservative consciousness of the importance of the problem of the recruitment of leadership is especially needed in the United States where many people have been deluding themselves into acceptance of the myth that we have no elites. The writer doubts whether any society has ever existed without elites. The real issue is whether elites shall be recruited rationally or haphazardly.

In general, neo-conservatism is a reaction to the crisis of the present. *In neo-conservative terms, the essential characteristic of the contemporary world crisis is the spread of disorder—both on the intellectual and the social levels. On the intellectual level, the individual has been deprived of a grasp of the order of values by the spread of the twin forces of nihilism and equalitarianism. On the social plane, the individual has been deprived of the sense of membership in the social order. The result has been the rise to prominence of the rootless individual—the spiritual proletarian. The conservative remedy has been to revive and give contemporary relevance to the ideals of an elitist form of humanism. As regards the individual, the conservative formula for happiness embodies a life of productive achievement (the work ethic) supported by a sense of emotional security and regulated in terms of high standards of competitive excellence. In brief, the conservative thinks of evil in terms of fragmentation; good, in terms of order.*

Essentialists have generally been too utilitarian in their approach to realize the essentially spiritual nature of the contemporary world crisis. The perennialists have generally shown a consciousness of the need for an ordering of values but have largely neglected the problem of community and the need for traditional bonds to integrate the members of a given society. As we have seen, they have also generally not realized how much the deterioration of the standards of selective excellence in the face of a burgeoning equalitarianism has contributed to the present state of fragmentation and intellectual anarchy. The neo-conservatives have viewed the problem on a broader canvas than have their colleagues on the educational Right. To assert, as their opponents on the educational Center and Left have frequently done, that the ideas of the neo-conservatives lack contemporary relevance indicates a lack of understanding of the conservative method. The real question concerns the practicality of the solutions offered by the neo-conservatives. In this respect, the educational thought of the neo-conservatives assumes tremendous importance. By focusing on the very weaknesses in American education that have perplexed generations of European observers, the neo-conservatives might well have shown others the road to reform. This road must begin with the reassessment of the basic assumptions that have guided the educational process.

SELECTED
BIBLIOGRAPHY

Adler, Mortimer J. *The Difference of Man and the Difference It Makes*. New York: Holt, Rinehart, and Winston, 1967.

Auerbach, Morton. *The Conservative Illusion*. New York: Columbia University Press, 1959.

Babbitt, Irving, et al. *Criticism in America: Its Function and Status*. New York: Harcourt Brace, 1924.

————. *Literature and the American College*. Chicago: Henry Regnery, 1956.

————. *On Being Creative*. Boston: Houghton Mifflin, 1932.

————. *Rousseau and Romanticism*. New York: Meridian Books, 1955.

Bantock, G. H. *Education and Values*. London: Faber and Faber, 1965.

————. *Education, Culture, and the Emotions*. London: Faber and Faber, 1967.

————. *Education in an Industrial Society*. London: Faber and Faber, 1963.

————. *Freedom and Authority in Education*. London: Faber and Faber, 1955.

————. *T. S. Eliot and Education*. New York: Random House, 1969.

Becker, Ernest. *Beyond Alienation*. New York: George Braziller, 1967.

Bell, Bernard Iddings. *Crisis in Education*. New York: Whittlesey House, 1949.

————. *Crowd Culture*. Chicago: Henry Regnery, 1956.

Bestor, Arthur. *The Restoration of Learning*. New York: Alfred A. Knopf, 1955.

Bode, Boyd H. *How We Learn*. Boston: D. C. Heath, 1940.

Brameld, Theodore. *Patterns of Educational Philosophy*. New York: Holt, Rinehart, and Winston, 1971.

Burke, Edmund. *On the Sublime and the Beautiful*. New York: P. F. Collier and Son, 1937.

————. *Reflections on the Revolution in France*. New York: Liberal Arts Press, 1955.

Calleo, David P., *Coleridge and the Idea of the Modern State*. New Haven: Yale University Press, 1960.

Canavan, Francis P., S. J. *The Political Reason of Edmund Burke*. Durham: Duke University Press, 1960.

Chapman, Gerald V. *Edmund Burke: The Practical Imagination*. Cambridge Mass.: Harvard University Press, 1969.

Chapman, Philip C. "The New Conservatism: Cultural Criticism versus Political Philosophy," *The Political Science Quarterly* 76 (March, 1960) 17-34.

Eliot, T. S. *After Strange Gods*. New York: Harcourt Brace, 1934.

————. *The Idea of a Christian Society*. New York: Harcourt Brace, 1940.

————. *Knowledge and Experience in the Philosophy of F. H. Bradley*. London: Faber and Faber, 1964.

————. *Notes Towards the Definition of Culture*. New York: Harcourt Brace, 1949.

————. *Selected Essays*. New York: Harcourt Brace and World, 1960.

————. *To Criticize the Critic and Other Essays*. New York: Farrar, Straus, and Giroux, 1965.

————. *What is a Classic?* London: Faber and Faber, 1945.

Elyot, Sir Thomas. *The Book Named the Governor*. London: Dent, 1962.

Fletcher, John Gould, et al. *I'll Take My Stand*. New York: Harper and Row, 1962.

Foerster, Norman, ed. *Humanism and America*. New York: Farrar and Rinehart, 1930.

Grattan, C. Hartley, ed. *The Critique of Humanism*. New York: Brewer and Warren, 1930.

Hemenway, Robert, ed. *A Great Books Primer*. Chicago: Great Books Foundation, 1955.

Hofstadter, Richard. *Anti-Intellectualism in American Life*. New York: Alfred A. Knopf, 1963.

Hogg, Quintin. *The Case for Conservatism*. Harmondsworth: Penguin Books, 1947.

Hooker, Richard. *Of the Laws of the Ecclesiastical Polity*. London: Dent, 1907.

Hutchins, Robert M. "T. S. Eliot on Education," *Measure* 1 (Winter, 1950): 1-8.

Josephson, Eric, and Mary, eds. *Man Alone*. New York: Dell, 1964.

Karier, Clarence J. *Man, Society, and Education*. Chicago: Scott, Foresman, 1967.

Kendall, Willmoore. *The Conservative Affirmation*. Chicago: Henry Regnery, 1963.

Kennedy, Gail, ed. *Education for Democracy*. Boston: Heath, 1952.

Kirk, Russell. *Academic Freedom*. Chicago: Henry Regnery, 1955.

———. *Beyond the Dreams of Avarice*. Chicago: Henry Regnery, 1956.

———. *The Conservative Mind*. Chicago: Henry Regnery, 1953.

———. *Eliot and His Age*. New York: Random House, 1971.

———. *A Program for Conservatives*. Chicago: Henry Regnery, 1962.

Kojecky, Roger. *T. S. Eliot's Social Criticism*. London: Faber and Faber, 1971.

Kunitz, Stanley J. and Haycraft, Howard, eds. *Twentieth Century Authors*. New York: H. W. Wilson, 1942.

Leander, Folke. *Humanism and Naturalism*. Goteborg: Wettergren and Kerbers Forlag, 1937.

Lewis, Gordon K. "The Metaphysics of Conservatism," *The Western Political Quarterly* 6 (December, 1953): 728-741.

Lovejoy, Arthur O. *The Great Chain of Being*. New York: Harper and Row, 1960.

McKean, Keith F. *The Moral Measure of Literature*. Denver: Alan Swallow, 1961.

Manchester, Frederick and Shepherd, Odell, eds. *Irving Babbitt: Man and Teacher*. New York: Putnam, 1941.

Mercier, Louis J. A. *The Challenge of Humanism*. New York: Oxford University Press, 1933.

Mills, C. Wright. *The Power Elite*. New York: Oxford University Press, 1956.

More, Paul Elmer. *Aristocracy and Justice*. Boston: Houghton Mifflin, 1915.

Nash, Paul; Kazamias, Andreas M., and Perkinson, Henry J., eds. *The Educated Man*. New York: Wiley, 1965.

Newman, John Henry, Cardinal. *The Idea of a University*. London: Longman's Green, 1923.

Nisbet, Robert A. *Community and Power*. New York: Oxford University Press, 1962.

—————. *The Sociological Tradition*. New York: Basic Books, 1966.

Northrop, F. S. C. *The Meeting of East and West*. New York: Collier Books, 1948.

Parkin, Charles. *The Moral Basis of Burke's Political Thought*. Cambridge: Cambridge University Press, 1956.

Phillips, Norman R. "The Conservative Implications of Skepticism," *The Journal of Politics* 18 (February, 1956): 28-38.

—————. "Genetics and Political Conservatism," *The Western Political Quarterly* 12 (September, 1959): 753-762.

—————. "An Historical Understanding of Conservatism," *The National Review* 21 (March 25, 1969): 279-281, 297.

—————. "The Role of Conservatism Today," *Modern Age* 7 (Summer, 1963): 242-248.

Pratte, Richard. *Contemporary Theories of Education*. Scranton: Intext Educational Publishers, 1971.

Rosenberg, Bernard and White, David Manning, eds. *Mass Culture*. New York: Free Press, 1957.

Rossiter, Clinton. *Conservatism in America: The Thankless Persuasion*. 2nd ed. New York: Vintage Books, 1962.

Schuettinger, Robert L., ed. *The Conservative Tradition in European Thought*. New York: Putnam, 1970.

Sigmund, Paul E. *Natural Law in Political Thought*. Cambridge, Mass.: Winthrop, 1971.

Stanlis, Peter J. *Edmund Burke and the Natural Law*. Ann Arbor: University of Michigan Press, 1958.

Viereck, Peter. *Conservatism: From John Adams to Churchill*. Princeton: Van Nostrand, 1956.

Vivas, Eliseo. *The Moral Life and the Ethical Life*. Chicago: University of Chicago Press, 1950.

Voegelin, Eric. *Science, Politics, and Gnosticism*. Chicago: Henry Regnery, 1968.

Weaver, Richard. *The Ethics of Rhetoric*. Chicago: Henry Regnery, 1968.

————. *Ideas Have Consequences*. Chicago: University of Chicago Press, 1948.

————. "The Image of Culture," *Modern Age* 8 (September, 1964): 186-199.

————. "The Importance of Cultural Freedom," *Modern Age* 6 (Winter, 1961-1962): 21-34.

White, R. J., ed. *The Conservative Tradition*. New York: New York University Press, 1957.

Wynne, John P. *Theories of Education*. New York: Harper and Row, 1963.

Zoll, Donald A. "Conservatism and a Philosophy of Personality," *Modern Age* 4 (Spring, 1960): 160-166.